I0062932

# BLUEPRINT FOR ALIGNED AND LEAN HEALTHCARE

## How to Create and Align Culture, Strategy and Operational Excellence Top to Bottom

Karl G. Kraber, MPA, MA ABS

Copyright ©2019 by Kata Consulting Services, LLC. All rights reserved. Printed in the United States of America. Except as permitted under the United States Copyright Act of 1976, no part of this publication may be reproduced or distributed in any form without permission of the copyright holder, except for brief quotations included in reviews and article, and the appendices, which are meant to serve as templates for the reader.

Print ISBN 978-0-578-58584-0

Ebook ISBN 978-0-578-58585-7

This book was written with the intent to educate, inform and instruct. This book contains information based upon real work environments. Reasonable efforts have been made to publish examples of real data and information, but the author used the data only for illustration purpose only and cannot assume responsibility for the validity of all materials or the consequences of their use. The author has attempted to trace the copyright holders of materials reproduced in this publication and has received written permission when major reference material was used. The author apologizes if permission to publish has not been obtained. If any copyright material has not been appropriately acknowledged, please write and let me know so I can fix it in any future reference or reprint.

**Copy Editor**

     Nathaniel Youmans

**Graphics Support**

     MikeDesignPro

**Cover Design**

     Bespoke Book Covers

**Cover Photo Courtesy of**

     McLaren Healthcare, Lansing, Michigan

# Table of Contents

Preface

Most books I've read about Lean methods have seemed like they were describing either the architecture of a building without the plumbing, or the plumbing without the architecture. The purpose of this book is to offer both the big picture architecture and some of the finer details (plumbing, electrical, HVAC, and framing, for instance). While this is not meant to be a comprehensive treatise on all methods and tools, my intent is to provide a blueprint that addresses the high-level conceptual and strategic thinking, as well as the day-to-day operations of front-line staff with patients (aka customers). Where I believe it would be useful to the reader, I go into deeper explanations of some of these strategic process improvement tools.

I wrote this book to serve two purposes: first, to give myself a guide to follow in the future, one that captures lessons I've learned and discoveries I've made—essentially, it is a long checklist. This project also serves a second purpose: to give my colleagues and their clients the same kind of informational guide. It took me many years to piece together an architecture that works effectively. I needed to answer questions such as: Do I start with projects – to prove the value of Lean? Do I start at the top or the bottom of the organization with Lean events and methods? How do I help my clients (administrators, clinical managers, service departments, etc.) prioritize where to commit their resources? Should we develop a strategy that can be deployed and used to guide the rest of the work? What if the executives do not see the value of strategic planning? If they do, what is the best structure to use?

It has only been over the last few years that I've had a chance to work at every level of an organization, with both the vertical connections and horizontal interdependencies as it relates to their objectives and measures. In this case, it was a hospital system.

This book, then, is an attempt to describe the structure, or blueprint, that I used.[1] Since first drafting it, I have followed my own blueprint in a state government setting, and achieved the same results as before, but more quickly, since I had a plan to follow. I have written this book primarily for experienced practitioners and leaders who wish to strategically and operationally align their organization with Lean and Lean-like tools to create a more efficient, effective hospital. It is my hope that you will experience the same desirable results sooner, as I did, by following this guidebook.

I do not necessarily go into detailed justification about why an organization should implement Lean or process improvement. Other books do a great job of justifying organizational improvement through Lean and other processes. It is assumed that the reader already knows the for such improvement methodologies.

In this book, I lay out a set of principles, methods, and tools that a) serve to align an organization toward its mission, vision, core values, strategies, and goals; b) create or identify existing mechanisms to manage and monitor progress toward those strategies, goals, and objectives in a way that will translate from top to bottom; and c) provide a means for frontline staff — the subject matter experts, to fully engage in meeting those objectives.

I reference and describe several of these tools and methods throughout the book. As mentioned before, my intent is to present a basic structure to which several tools could be applied. This is not to say that these are the only tools you can use. However, if you do use these tools, they will work.

In essence, this book defines how to effectively start the "Lean" journey. Like creating a healthy lifestyle based holistically on body, personality, and environment, organizations must try different improvement tools and approaches, making adjustments for their culture and structure. That said, the critical success factors that apply to any organization are: a) ensure engaged and visible

---

[1] Thank you, Gracie Tena de Lara, for giving me the idea for using this term.

leadership, b) have a clear, articulable structure and pathway by which to meet goals, and 3) STICK TO IT!

Tenacity, perseverance, discipline, and "constancy of purpose," to use Dr. W. Edwards Deming's term, are all more important than the specific approach you select. Adjust your approach as you learn from its application. I'm sure you recall the four-step Deming cycle: Plan, Do, Check, and Adjust. I contend that Check and Adjust are the most important steps of the cycle because they demonstrate that you are truly learning. You check to see if your "solution" was effective. No matter how well your solution worked, or didn't, you will learn from these experiences and adjust accordingly. Your adjustment is your direct evidence of learning, and learning is *everything* in a Lean environment.

One last note: I am not a medical professional or clinician. That will be obvious throughout the book. I've used that to my advantage: I could ask the "dumb" questions no one else would dare. My strengths, as a Lean expert, are bringing a fresh set of eyes to the work, asking questions only a non-clinician can ask, and providing the tools needed to accomplish goals. That said, one of my best experiences was pairing with a former ED director as a co-facilitator of a week-long workshop. She brought depth of knowledge and asked insightful questions. I brought the clarity of not being hampered by preconceived notions about how hospitals work. In turn, I got to ask a lot of questions that caused the clinicians to get past the knee-jerk "that's just the way it's always been done here" reaction. Besides, a facilitator is not going to solve your problems. They can, however, guide your staff and empower them with the tools to do so themselves.

## Acknowledgements

I am indebted to two people in particular for their help and advice on this book. First to Graciela Tena de Lara who provided a critical eye on the shaping of the book and unfailing support in its development.

Secondly, Mark Dean, who gave one of the most in-depth reviews of the book, and provided many insights and questions that resulted in my rewriting major sections of the book. Thanks to both of you.

Also, thank you to Paul O'Mara and the three reviewers at ASQ who gave me critical guidance on the content and format of this book. Your feedback has been invaluable.

The cover photo is courtesy of McLaren General Lansing hospital in Lansing, Michigan, my last client before publishing this book. A great group of people who've helped me validate several of the concepts, principles, and tools described in these pages.

Finally, thank you to my wife, Tuyen, whose everlasting support makes life's journey that much more fun.

# Chapter 1 — Creating a Lean Culture

### Starting with Culture

Lean ultimately starts with culture, and Lean culture is defined by *respect for people* and *continuous improvement*. *Respect for people* means to honor their skills, knowledge, and experience by engaging them in problem solving, process improvement, and developing service delivery and quality care. Lean culture involves not only engaging team members in a respectful way, but also challenging them to ever-higher levels of performance, confident that they will rise to the challenge.

*Continuous improvement* has two aspects to it. The first is the philosophical belief that we should always be improving our people, processes, products, services, etc. The second aspect of *continuous improvement* comes down to the fact that it is our visible behaviors that constitute the Lean culture. That is, we are trying to improve our culture by changing our behaviors.

The predominant Western view of Lean is this: projects, workshops, quality circles, and Kanban boards. The main reason most organizations implement Lean is to increase efficiency through the reduction of waste, and to improve effectiveness, services, and products through best practices.

This picture of Lean has been painted a thousand times in as many organizations that have attempted to implement it. Why, then, do attempts to implement Lean tend to fail? Because the focus tends to be on the wrong things: conducting workshops. Often, we conduct workshops to reduce costs. This approach is similar to being "on a diet" to lose weight. We often achieve some short-term weight loss, but then the weight goes back on in time. What we want instead is for people to live a healthy lifestyle, which results in appropriate weight loss. A lifestyle change is long-lasting, unlike a diet, which is generally abandoned as time passes by. Lifestyle change, however, is harder, and takes a much more comprehensive approach.

Likewise, Lean culture is not about events. Lean culture is about the actions we take, big and small, every day and all day, to incrementally improve ourselves and our work environment. It is what we *do* every day, and this takes drive and discipline. An organization that successfully implements Lean does not relent in its ongoing improvement efforts. A manager I knew once had the following epiphany: "I thought Lean was about results. It's not. Lean is about action." Yes!

We have to get past the expectation that we can increase efficiency and efficacy by decree or by events only. Too many organizations seem to believe that if leadership says, "Reduce linen usage by 20%," that it will magically happen. It will not. Certainly not in the long run. Too many organizations, too, seem to think that if a manager believes they have the solution to a problem and mandates its use, that everyone will see the manager's wisdom and will fully support and sustain the solution. This will happen if and *only* if the manager is on the floor all the time to make sure it is followed.

Additionally, an executive might often say, "We have a problem. Let's have a workshop and fix it." That is not to say that events and workshops do not help. They can be enormously useful to bring together the right players to solve a problem relatively quickly. I frequently use workshops as a way to kick-start an organization

11

toward a respect-for-people and continuous-improvement mentality by teaching and helping them develop the skills of improvement. But we can't be so dependent on such workshops.

In my opinion, the book that best describes the profound significance of continuous improvement and respect for people is *The Toyota Way* by Jeffrey K. Liker.[2] He explores the unseen rules at Toyota that govern everyone's behavior, from top leadership to frontline mechanics. By "unseen," I mean that when Americans visit Toyota to learn about what they call the Toyota Production System (TPS), they see the tools and methods of what we might call Lean, but they tend to miss the underlying value system that allows Toyota's Lean culture to function so well. In other words, what we call Lean, they call the TPS. As Liker describes it,

> The power behind TPS is a company's management commitment to continuously invest in its people and promote a culture of continuous improvement. (Liker, 2004)

The patriarch of the Toyota dynasty, Sakichi Toyoda, instilled these two primary values, continuous improvement and respect for people, among his heirs. Most of us rightfully construe respect for people as being nice to each other and treating everyone with respect and dignity. While this is certainly true to a degree, Toyoda's philosophy was more nuanced: respecting people involves both investing in their growth and learning, and challenging them to ever higher levels of excellence and success. This means setting high standards, and expecting people to meet them through the application of their skills, knowledge, and experience. Which brings us back to continuous improvement. The emphasis on respect and continuous improvement means that employees are coached and that their development is encouraged on an ongoing basis. For example, planning for future leadership succession means growing future leaders from within.

---

[2] Liker, Jeffrey K. *The Toyota Way*. McGraw-Hill, 2004.

12

Put another way, if we respect people and engage them to apply their knowledge, skills and experience, and if we strive to continuously improve and invest in developing people to greater levels of excellence, then we will see reduction of waste in the process. We will also get improvements in equipment, product design, quality of services, and development of new products, processes, and even space use and building design, as well.

More broadly then, Lean is about the continuous improvement of our work and our very being. Developing our people prepares them for continuous improvement in a wonderful upward spiral. Learning is the true focus of Lean, and it is a two-fold process of learning through experimentation ("Plan" and "Do"), and learning based upon what worked and what didn't ("Check" and "Adjust"). Making "scientists" of everyone is essentially the ultimate goal. Scientists, it could be argued, have the greatest learning potential, because their life's work is an endless process of trying, failing, learning, succeeding, learning, and repeating. A good medical professional will understand this.

In addition to Liker's *The Toyota Way*, I recommend reading Mike Rother's *Toyota Kata*.[3] In Japanese, *kata* means form. Rother deftly describes the critical value of continuous improvement in terms of Toyota's structure and form, and applies that understanding to the Lean journey. The book provides insights about the inner practices and disciplines of Toyota and its culture of continuous learning. So profound was the book on my thinking that I named my consulting firm, Kata Consulting Services, LLC, after it. Of katas, Kevin Malone says,

> Each major style of karate has innumerable katas which are designed to reflect the basic elements of that style. Within each style there are also groupings of related katas that share a similar structure and focus on a specific set of skills. Within these groupings, and within the style as a whole, there is usually a well-defined progression from one kata or group of katas to the

[3] Rother, Mike. *Toyota Kata*. McGraw-Hill, 2010.

next. Students are taught katas in an order that helps them build upon and enhance their basic skill.

When individuals first become karate students, they are introduced to a complete set of new skills. New students are taught basic techniques, but they need a training structure to learn how to use them effectively. Katas are an important part of helping these students develop their first awareness of how the techniques they are learning can be used in a fight. Later, as students rise through their school ranks, the katas can become more elaborate to meet the growing need to challenge the students to improve their skills.[4]

A Lean culture parallels this kata structure of karate. That is, it takes the form of standardized and stabilized processes, offers formalized problem-solving steps, and provides incremental learning in regards to the many forms and functions of collaborative and consensus decision-making.

Intuitively, we all practice some form of kata. I believe that everyone is a Lean or Kaizen practitioner at some level, though they might not know it. Who tries to find the shortest, fastest, and most reliable way to get from one place to another? Everyone. Why? To save gas, time, and wear and tear on the car and the driver. In other words, to reduce waste. Who, in trying to find the shortest, fastest and most reliable way, will try different methods (GPS, MapQuest, friends, Google Map, paper maps) until they settle on one route? Just about everyone. And who, after standardizing and stabilizing this route, will continue to seek out a new, even shorter, faster, more

---

[4] Malone, Kevin, 'Meaning of Kata,' *Blackrock Karate Club*, 13 August, 2004, http://homepage.eircom.net/~nmalone/meaning.htm.

reliable way? If your answer is "me," then you are already on the Lean pathway.

Taking this example further: if you were going to tell a friend how to get to your house, and had to choose between either the shortest, fastest route or the most reliable, which directions would you give? Every person that I have asked has answered "the most reliable," that is, the most predictable outcome. Predictability, then, comes from standardized practices. Standards, in turn, are the cornerstone of Lean (and Kaizen) process improvement, because they provide predictability. As Taiichi Ohno once said, "Without standards, there can be no Kaizen."

It makes one wonder. If this is so intuitive, then why don't we naturally create standard work at work? The answer is – we do! But only for ourselves. Getting everyone to agree on one standard turns out to be a bit more difficult.

On Creating Culture

Think about creating a Lean culture the same way as nurturing a child into a healthy, productive citizen. We are simultaneously helping them to accumulate knowledge and useful experiences, while ensuring their physical needs are being met, while also wrapping them in a loving and caring environment. All of this is incremental and long-term. We can't just throw them a birthday party and declare "You are loved!" and move on. However, increasing your chances of ensuring a healthy adult requires the right climate in which each contributing component needs to be present and persistent. Not doing so is akin to having one Lean workshop and declaring, "We are improved!" That may sound silly, but I know organizations who do essentially the same thing and wonder why they have cynical and disengaged employees.

Culture is created by what we believe and do. What we do shapes what we believe. Focus on the *doing* and the *believing*, and culture will follow. For example, by observing what families do during holidays, we get a pretty good idea about which beliefs and values are important to them. The same is true for observing behaviors in different societies to determine their social mores, values, beliefs, customs, etc. What people do in large part defines their culture; changing what we do, even in the most nuanced ways, say, during the holidays, changes our beliefs and values, and vice-versa. Why the increasing outcry against the over-commercialization of Christmas? Because everyone is out shopping. What we *do* can actually override our values and, in turn, re-shape those values. This is not to say the argument is as simple as *believe* versus *do*. In reality, they both inform one another, though we often underestimate the power of changing behaviors to change our values and attitudes.

The power of changing what we believe by changing how we behave is explained by the cognitive dissonance theory by Leon Festinger.[5] According to Festinger, cognitive dissonance theory is founded on the assumption that individuals seek consistency between their expectations and their reality—between what they think and what they actually do. Because of this, people engage in a process called "dissonance reduction" in order to bring their cognitions and actions in line with one another. Creating this uniformity, then, lessens the psychological tension and distress.

If there is dissonance between how people behave and what they believe, and they can't change how they behave, then their belief system must compensate and adjust. Think about the changes in the past fifty years in our culture's attitude toward smoking.[6] Starting in 1964, many public service announcements came out about how bad smoking was. Pretty soon, changes in packaging were implemented, which appeared to reflect this shifting societal attitude toward smoking and its adverse health effects. Reduction

---

[5] Festinger, Leon. *A Theory of Cognitive Dissonance.* Stanford University Press, 1957.
[6] Cummings, K. Michael and Robert N. Proctor. "The Changing Public Image of Smoking in the United States: 1964-2014." *Cancer Epidemiology, Biomarkers & Prevention: A Publication of the American Association for Cancer Research, Cosponsored by the American Society of Preventative Oncology.* United States National Library of Medicine, National Institutes of Health. Volume 23, Number 1. (2014): 32-36.

in smoking occurred, but we didn't experience the biggest change in social attitudes until the 1970s and 1980s, when smoking became prohibited on planes, in working environments, public buildings, certain parks, and, now, within 25 feet from a window or door. People I know who smoke don't even smoke in their own homes! There was a 180-degree attitude switch throughout the country over the public image of smoking, but it took a few decades for this transition to occur.

What is this leading to? If you want to change the culture of your organization, first, you must be clear about what you want that new culture to look like, and then you must define the behaviors that constitute it. Concurrently, you must also define the activities that will reinforce those behaviors and cultural attributes. The vision and expectations of the new culture must be declared and publicized, but accountability for *behavior* is more important than actual results, because the results will naturally follow.

I believe practitioners must explicitly engage leadership in a discussion about the culture they want to create, even if it is to focus on only a few key attributes that they can all agree are important to them. Do they place safety, the patient, or engaged staff first? Do they place profit above all else? People act in accordance with what is important to them, and what is important to them is often driven by incentives, either internal (living one's values) or external (bonuses for improved results and performance). The only way to ensure that everyone is working toward the same goal is if leadership agrees first upon the behaviors necessary to drive their desired culture, and then upon what the intrinsic and extrinsic incentives will be to support them.

Do not assume that such goals and visions are inherently known. They must be clearly stated. Organizational leaders often say they are changing their culture, but when asked toward what end, there is usually no clear answer. That is because everyone assumes we are all on the same page about the culture we want. This is, of course, rarely the case.

17

The new cultural model must be incorporated into everything you do: strategy, internal communication, initiatives, and so on. The cultural model does not need to be publicized externally, unless it makes marketing sense, but it needs to be widely disseminated internally. Be sure to hire, develop, and fire staff based on matching the desirable behaviors for the culture your organization wants to achieve.

If you want a safety-first culture, then there need to be safety events, safety huddles, safety measures, recognition for safe practices, and disciplinary action for employees not following safety rules. When safety is the first topic on the agenda, and when we go over the statistics to discuss how to fix any safety problems we are experiencing, *then* safety is clearly first. Otherwise, it is all so much talk.

One day, I was driving down a back street just outside of Jackson, Mississippi, in late summer of 2014, near, but not at, the end of the work day. I saw several adults playing volleyball. I realized I was driving by the offices of Blue Cross/Blue Shield of Mississippi (BC/BSMS), and was immediately reminded of a conversation I had had with a co-worker who said her husband worked there. "They really believe in supporting the health and wellness of their employees," she said. "They even have them play sports together during the day to stay in shape." That certainly seemed to be the case. Now, *that* is culture in action.

Why Is Change So Difficult?

Force of habit. We have so many mechanisms that support staying in our old habits. Not only do environmental factors (systems, structures, co-workers, incentives, and muscle memory) conspire to maintain the status quo, but our body and brain are actually wired to maintain a state of homeostasis. Homeostasis is the property of a system by which variables are regulated so that internal conditions remain stable and relatively constant. In his book *Mastery—The Keys to Success and Long-Term Fulfillment*, George

18

Leonard[7] describes how homeostasis affects our behavior and our sense of who we are. He states that homeostasis will prevent our body from making drastic changes and maintain stability in our lives even if it is detrimental to us. An 9example Leonard uses is an unstable family in which the father has been a raging alcoholic, then suddenly stops, and then his son starts up a drug habit to maintain stability in the family. Homeostasis is the main factor that stops people from changing their habits because our bodies resist change unless it is very slow.

As Tom Peters said, "People don't resist change. They resist being changed!"[8] Who hasn't resisted the changes that someone else wants to impose upon us? We know we should stop (fill in blank here), but just because someone else gives us the "good advice" to stop, that doesn't mean we're going to! However, we increase the likelihood of our commitment to change by seeking and gaining the support and involvement of everybody in the workplace who will be affected not only by the change itself, but also the actual *creation* of that change. Put another way, they buy in because change was happening *with* them, not *to* them.

Similarly, creating a new culture and implementing Lean projects are intertwined. A very common mistake by leaders and Lean practitioners alike is failing to recognize the two-way relationship in which projects create culture and culture reinforces the values and purposes of such projects. I have often seen everyone focused on just doing projects. It is not about the importance of individual projects, per se, but rather that they provide a means for training both staff and managers to negotiate, compromise, plan for action, and sustain change.

Facilitative Leader or Leader as Coach

---

[7] Leonard, George. *Mastery—The Keys to Success and Long-Term Fulfillment*. Plume, 1992.

[8] Peter, Tom. *Passion for Excellence*. Grand Central Publishing, 1989.

Managers must shift their perspectives and their relationships to subordinates, and this shift must be geared toward producing a facilitative leader who guides the work team through problem solving and process improvement. This includes all aspects of operations, from how to reduce falls, hand-off time, and operating room turnover rate, to preventing hospital-acquired conditions and medical errors, to improving the quality of care, sanitation, equipment maintenance, and so on. So-called projects give everyone the opportunity to practice new roles and rules of engagement.

At the hospital where I worked, we started our journey as most organizations do: project by project. But by convincing everyone of the value and positive impact of our Lean work, we added an element to the projects that began to make them more than "just projects." These were the beginnings of our cultural shift. We coached the hospital presidents, vice-presidents, directors, clinical managers, and supervisors in the five hospitals on their roles and responsibilities—not just for Lean projects, but for how their hierarchical relationships should play out with *any* project, too.

We explored the extent to which administrators and supervisors, rather than micro-manage, trusted their staff to know how to make level-appropriate decisions. If they didn't trust their staff, then why? Was it a competency issue? A reliability issue? How can they train, coach, and develop their subordinates to be trustworthy and dependable?

We also worked with the managers and leaders to create an environment of experimentation and learning, rather than blaming. What if there was no fault to be found, but, rather, procedural and structural problems that needed to be identified, analyzed and resolved? This began to free people's hearts and minds to work on improving service-delivery, instead of hiding mistakes or problems for fear of being blamed.

A fundamental belief in Lean is that people are doing the best job they can, given the processes and systems with which they have to work. If those processes and systems are broken, then the outcome (the organization's products and services) will also be broken.

Blaming employees for problems caused by broken, inefficient processes is akin to blaming the driver for a bumpy ride on a pothole-ridden road.

Another avenue we pursued in changing organizational culture was to mandate that every person in a management position, from supervisor up, attend a Facilitative Leadership Training course. We took the Lean facilitation course and changed about 1% of the content from instructing facilitators to instructing "facilitative leaders." The difference between the two is subtle but distinct. In fact, we often had facilitators-in-training in the same class. We emphasized that the difference between the two was that a facilitative leader had content-investment, but was expected to ask questions, rather than give answers, and the facilitator was expected to be entirely content-neutral.


Tipping Point

Frequently, shifting culture can be greatly enhanced by creating a catalyst that dramatically changes attitudes and behaviors. This usually means tapping into something that has significance to those in the organization. We stumbled upon a tipping-point moment for shifting the nurses' attitude toward accepting Lean.

At one of our hospitals, one of the nurse managers was enrolled in a Master's degree program that required a Lean project. She decided to use the 5S method (sort, simplify, sweep, standardize and sustain) to organize her unit's clinical supply room. It was so successful and easy to find supplies that the nurses on the adjacent floors discovered it was faster to travel to the next floor than it was to get supplies from their own respective floors. You can imagine the dismay of the managers when they discovered one floor was supplying the needs of three.

Soon, the director required nursing managers on each floor (a total of nine) to use 5S when organizing their own supply rooms. The floors did not act independently: standardized color categories and supply lists were created, and adjustments were made for types of clinical areas like Med/Surg, ICU, PCU, etc. Then, the presidents of all five hospitals in the system agreed to implement the same changes.

Three important results came out this activity that produced the tipping point. First, everyone was happy with how easy it had become to find supplies. Second, material management staff could better monitor supplies and inventory, so the supply room's percent availability exceeded 98%. And third, the nurses wrestled control of their supply room away from material management and into their own hands. Even though the nurses were, in effect, customers of the material management department, this change gave them power over their own work environment that they had never had before. Not surprisingly, one nurse told me enthusiastically, "We like this!"

Six Sources of Influence: Tools to Support Culture Change

One of the perioperative nursing managers had read the book *Influencer: The Power to Change Anything*, and got the word out about how useful it was .[9] Upon reading it myself, I realized that it served as a great resource for checking to see whether we were attending to the six sources of influence that would help us strengthen our culture-shift effort. *Influencer*, it turned out, provided one of the most easily-understood descriptive *and* prescriptive and models that I have encountered to support cultural change. See Illustration 1.1.

---

[9]McMillan, Ron, et al. *Influencer: The Power to Change Anything*. McGraw-Hill Education, 2008.

# Six Sources of Influence

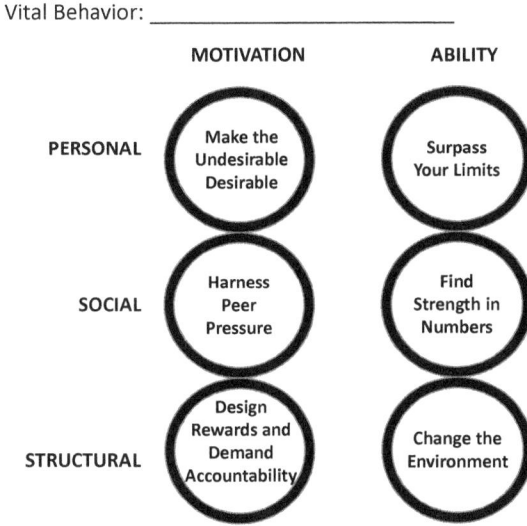

Vital Behavior: _____

|  | MOTIVATION | ABILITY |
|---|---|---|
| PERSONAL | Make the Undesirable Desirable | Surpass Your Limits |
| SOCIAL | Harness Peer Pressure | Find Strength in Numbers |
| STRUCTURAL | Design Rewards and Demand Accountability | Change the Environment |

Illustration 1.1 Six Sources of Influence Model

*Influencer* addresses all the requirements needed not only to make large-scale organizational change, but also to sustain that change by addressing the individual, group, and institutional strategies that will ensure the sustainability of such improvements.

Below is a simplified explanation of a very elegant model. I strongly encourage the reader to go to the book for a wonderful and detailed explanation of this model. My explanation, however, is a lead-in to how we have used this tool to support our culture change and, specifically, to change behaviors toward that culture. In *Influencer*, the authors show, through example after example, how behavior changes only after people believe that it is worth it, and when they realize that they can do it.

The book emphasizes having a clear, concise description of the new behavior (called a "Vital Behavior") you want people to adopt. This Vital Behavior needs to be easily understood by all, and, more

23

importantly, actionable by everyone. For example, the Vital Behavior might be as straight forward as "Wash hands between patients." If we are clear about the new behavior we want people to adopt, then we assess and identify the motivation and ability of the individual, groups and the organization to influence everyone to implement this new behavior.

The six sources are divided as:

1. Personal Motivation: *Is this new behavior worth it?*
2. Personal Ability: *Can I do it?*
3. Social Motivation: *How do we make doing it acceptable and NOT doing it unacceptable?*
4. Social Ability: *What can we do to ensure that everyone can do it?*
5. Structural Motivation: *Are there systems or cues in our environment that make it worth it to me/us?*
6. Structural Ability: *Does our environment enable us to reasonably accomplish this new behavior?*

Where I deviate from the specifics of this model is in the Vital Behaviors. I do this because the Strategic Priorities are more complex than a single statement, but the overall model guides us toward answering key questions to ensure we approach the organization systemically and methodically. Doing this requires reshaping some of the questions we would ask ourselves, as described below. Where this description is consistent with the *Influencer* model on Vital Behaviors is that many of the projects and initiatives can, by themselves, be distilled into Vital Behaviors.

"Provide the right service to the right patient at the right time" became our default Vital Behavior because, as an overall statement, it was relevant to the mission of the whole organization, with variations on this theme depending on the department. For example, material management adapted this to be, "Provide the right supply to the right patient, at the right time."

## Personal Motivation—Make the Undesirable Desirable

*How do we help people adopt a Vital Behavior? Do they all believe it is worth it?*

Masterful influencers find ways of connecting people's actions to their personal values. The ability to connect one's actions to their broader values, for example, can be a greater predictor of whether an addict will give up their addictive habits. In our context, though, we asked questions of our staff: what do they want? Why do they want it? By connecting the behaviors to desired outcomes, you begin to replace judgment with empathy.

**Questions we asked:**

Why are we taking this strategic journey? How does that translate to the individual? Why should they care?

**What we did to answer these questions:**

During training and department meetings we asked staff about their best customer service experiences. We then asked if they thought we met those expectations with patient service. "No" was the usual response. Follow-up questions included, "do you believe that you individually can make a difference in the experience of a patient?"

"Yes."

"Do you believe that a patient having a consistent and successful experience will occur if everyone works in concert with each other?"

"Yes."

Referring back to the excellent experience they had, we explored standardizing work practices as a critical element of providing that service. This was tied into the overall strategic objective of standardized processes, practices, and procedures. Our work with the team was to develop those standards for each service line or department.

**Surpass Your Limits**

## Personal Ability — Surpass Your Limits

*How do we help people adopt a Vital Behavior? Can they do it?*

We often underestimate the need to practice. We make the assumption that if we explain something once or the behavior is tried once, then it is mastered. Practice is essential to mastering any skill, and we often shortcut the need to practice, especially when it's a soft skill.

Facilitative leadership is exactly the type of soft skill managers must learn in order to successfully attain and then sustain the work defined in this model. Facilitative leadership is the ability for a manager to use interpersonal skills such as asking questions, paraphrasing, summarizing, enquiring, focusing conversation, etc., within their own workgroup. An example of this would be a manager facilitating their workgroup's operation's huddle. The importance of the skill set is evidenced in watching managers who failed miserably at getting issues resolved because they didn't know how to engage staff to do the work, take the initiative, and close the deal.

Deliberate Practice is Necessary:
- Demand full attention for brief intervals
- Provide immediate feedback against a clear standard
- Break mastery into mini-goals
- Prepare for set-backs and view as opportunity to learn

- Share timely and accurate data/feedback that supports the vital changes you are making
- Practice, practice, practice

**Questions we asked:**

What do employees need to do differently? What training, education and experiences can we give them to enable them to meet expectations? Will they learn better in smaller groups, for example a 1:5 teacher to student ratio, rather than 1:25?

**What we did to answer these questions:**

We created a five-day class to teach leaders meeting management, change management, facilitative leadership, and Lean concepts. There were several opportunities throughout the five days to *practice* the skills we were teaching. The last day was an inpatient simulation that included frontline staff who were going to be team members. The inpatient simulation provided participants with an opportunity to learn and practice several Lean concepts, including the Daily Management Board huddle (which will be described in Chapter 3). The emphasis was on participation and teamwork. All had a chance to practice the role they would be called upon to fulfill during team meetings and workshops, the extended events, huddles, and impromptu problem-solving sessions.

**Harness Peer Pressure**

Social Motivation—Harness Peer Pressure

*Who are the influencers? How can we engage them?*

Derek Sivers provides a fascinating study of the role of followers in a YouTube video called, "First Follower: Leadership Lessons from

27

Dancing Guy."[10]  It is an example of how important the peer role is to the success of the change wanted.

What starts off as a guy looking like a nut, dancing alone on a hill at a concert, reveals the social dynamic of making a lone nut into a leader.  The premise is that being the first person in a movement doesn't necessarily make someone a leader. Rather, it is only through the bravery of the next guy (the first follower) who follows the lone dancer.  In the act of following, and enlisting his own friends to join, the second dancer legitimizes the "nut" as a leader.

Then a shift occurs: what might have been judged first as crazy becomes the now-accepted new normal.  When one man danced alone, it became socially acceptable to join in the dance and, arguably, not socially acceptable to remain seated.  This is peer pressure at its most basic, and the video provides an important lesson: the number of peers does not have to be large. Even just one or two people can strongly influence opinion.

This dynamic is also subtly at play when there are two facilitators or trainers leading a group or workshop.  They both are simultaneously "first followers" to each other, implicitly validating what the other person is doing.  From now on, send two people out to introduce and train staff on the new standard work that will be used in the workplace.  The first follower dynamic will hold.

In our culture, we don't like to have people claim, "I'm in charge."  So, we have someone else introduce the new hospital president, manager, chief of staff, etc.  The one doing the introduction is automatically the first follower and legitimizes the new leader.

This is where Social Motivation, the desire of people to join in, intersects with Social Ability.  The leader and first follower clearly demonstrate what the new behavior looks like, and that it is, therefore, easy to follow.

---

[10] Derek Sivers, "First Follower: Leadership Lessons from Dancing Guy, Youtube video, 2:57, February 11, 2010, https://www.youtube.com/watch?v=fW8amMCVAJQ.

**Questions we asked:**

Who are the influencers? How can we engage them to become first followers? How do we engage the right staff in creating the expectations as a group? What is their collective vested interest? How do we create an environment among the staff that makes it not okay to opt out?

**What we did to answer these questions:**

We talked with managers and staff (team members) about who we should engage up front. The implementation plan included actions to engage influencers early on, before the rest of the unit. Trial runs of our proposed countermeasures and solutions also became opportunities for non-team members to participate. As team members went out to get feedback on standard work, they were coached about not blaming and not being defensive, so that an environment of experimentation could start to be created.

We set a precedent that two people would go teach, inform, and coach staff on new processes and procedures. This set up the implied leader/first follower dynamic without having to say who was who.

We had two facilitators supporting the staff teams as much as possible. Besides the opportunity to learn from each other and to better observe group dynamics, this two-person approach implied the understanding that, by their very presence, each facilitator was also following the lead of the other. We thusly modeled the tandem leader/follower dynamic.

**Find Strength in Numbers**

Social Ability — Find Strength in Numbers

*With whom can you connect or collaborate?*

You can't succeed on your own. This best describes Social Ability. It is the social capital needed to bring about big change. It is answering the question, "With whom can you connect or collaborate?" As in the first follower, we are seeking others in the unit to support and help us demonstrate what we hope will be the new normal.

Sense of community in creating a new normal can be very powerful. How do we move to a place where staff all hold each other accountable? What does that mean? What will you do when you see an opportunity to elevate an experience or performance to the next level? Can you imagine a place where we all commit to helping each other with these new behaviors? This is probably one of the biggest changes we asked of our staff: we wanted them to self-police, to hold each other accountable with timely, specific, and respectful feedback.

Leaders must be on board with holding people accountable, and they must be tenacious in doing so. They must also lead by example and be able to define *why* and demonstrate *how*. Leaders themselves, of course, have to be consistent, motivated, and willing to take critical feedback.

**Questions we asked:**

How do we create a safe team environment that allows individuals and groups the safety to fail and learn? What shared training, education and experience do we need to provide that encourages them to support and reinforce the required behavior — even in failure? What structures do we need in place at the process level to prevent regressing to old processes or outmoded behaviors?

**What we did to answer these questions:**

We also demonstrated, practiced and coached the training principle of the "Three Tells," which I learned in the United States Air Force:

- Tell' em what you're going to tell' em.

- Tell'em.
- Tell'em what you told'em."

If something is worth knowing, repeat it three times to make sure everyone has heard it at least once.

When we were introducing new protocols and standards, for example, we had always had two instructors who taught small groups, with no training session having more than eight people. Training was application-based and trainees had to sign or initial they understood and could apply with what they learned. Managers then had to follow-up to ensure the new standard was being met or protocol followed. Managers were coached to be exactly that: coaches, rather than "auditors." We suggested that they assume good intentions among their staff: that they want to do a good job, but need clarification and support. Questions we taught them to ask were: "What obstacles prevent you from doing this?" "How can I help remove those obstacles?" "Should I describe this differently?"

Other ways to help staff learn new behaviors include:

- Learn one, do one, teach one model — spread the standard and expectations among staff
- Find a coach and be a coach
- Make it safe not to know how to do it
- Make it uncomfortable to be the only one NOT doing a new behavior
- Never underestimate the power of GUILT!

Design
Rewards and
Demand
Accountability

31

## Structural Motivation — Design Rewards and Demand Accountability

*What set of positive and negative consequences do we need to establish in order to reward the right behavior and deter the wrong behavior?*

Too frequently, organizations take the easy way out by trying to create motivation by rewarding (through reward and recognition programs) or punishing people into submission (through disciplinary processes) as they implement the new behavior, procedure, or standard. While they are oftentimes necessary as part of an overall plan, both rewards and negative consequences should be the final, last-resort strategy. Build personal and social motivation first. If people do something just for the rewards they will stop doing it once rewards go away. We found that displaying team, and sometimes individual, performance in a visible location was a stronger motivator than thank you cards and Snickers bars (please see below for more on this).

Also, if you are going to reward, then reward *behaviors*, not just *results*. Remember, we are looking for a cultural change. We can show results by gaming the system without changing the fundamental behavior sought. An example of this is trying to get doctors to reduce "Door to Doc" time as part of an effort to reduce length of stay (LOS) in the emergency room. When rewards were put in place to see patients faster, doctors frequently ignored discharging patients in favor of seeing new patients, which had the unintended consequence of filling the ER to capacity, boarding patients, and increasing the length of stay!

The behavior we wanted was to continuously improve the flow of patients and reduce their length of stay. Unfortunately, because of our reward system, the results we got were more patients requiring a longer stay.

Holding people accountable for certain norms includes being aware of cause and effect. Think ahead about what will happen if changes don't occur. What will you do? Managing consequences for those who do not want to adjust to the new normal is critical.

32

You can send a powerful message when you hold others accountable. When all else (training, coaching, developing) fails, you may have to resort to disciplinary action or coaching-out. The intent of coaching-out is to help someone see that they will be happier elsewhere. In other words, choosing to get off the bus because one's personal beliefs and behaviors don't fit in. And, just as we want to hire well, there are times when the only real option is to fire well.

**Questions we asked:**

As an organization or workgroup, what can we do to motivate people to improve performance? What can we do to ensure we have the right people to improve performance?

**What we did to answer these questions:**

Trend charts were used extensively on the Daily Management Boards to show both individual and group performance. Some staff were more competitive in making their numbers better, but all were motivated to improve. There were also department celebrations when significant progress was made and when goals were achieved.

Performance on the Daily Management Board was supplemented by 1:1 coaching where deficiencies existed. New hires were selected for the right behaviors and attitude. Promotions were likewise based on the right behaviors and attitude. We expected and experienced about a 20% turnover, mostly voluntary. Having people leave because they don't want to participate in this is not unusual. In fact, it is often a welcomed opportunity for managers to replenish their workforce with the right people.

**Change the Environment**

## Structural Ability — Change the Environment

*What systems or structures do we need to have in place to prevent relapse to old behaviors?*

There must be physical reinforcement to cue or encourage us to make and sustain desired changes. In other words, we have to make the change both easy and unavoidable. What environmental cues do we have? The more people are aligned with the desired Vital Behavior, the more effective the structural change will be. I believe that this is the most powerful of the six influencers. If a structure or system is created that gives NO choice, it trumps the rest.

**Questions we asked:**

What changes can we make through IT? What kinds of spatial remodeling might help align staff with the new behavior? What changes to our visual environment can we make?

**What we did to answer these questions:**

As an example of changing the structure, we changed the medical records system used to admit patients from the Emergency Department to Inpatient Department so that the doctors could not enter "Care Complete" until all the required actions and fields were completed. To support having a nurse be the first contact in the emergency room, the ER counters were moved and rearranged so that that the RN would precede Registration as the first line of contact. Both groups participated in the redesign of the ER entrance.

One of my favorite physical changes that cost virtually no money was changing the card access to the central sterile supply room. Initially, anyone who worked in Periop had card access to the supply room. The card access was changed so that it was limited to only Materiel Management staff. A previously blocked supply room door

34

was unblocked, and a customer-service desk and counter, which physically kept others from entering the area, were placed immediately inside the supply room. The amount of supplies that stopped walking away was in the hundreds of thousands of dollars. It wasn't theft so much as people just used to grabbing what they needed for surgery without charging it. They figured it would get captured at the point of patient delivery and didn't realize the impact it had on stores. We also color coded all clinical supply rooms to make it easier to find and restock supplies.

One final example that is a mix of both social and structural changes. Emergency room bed requests had to contain all of the required patient information to be entered into the bed request system by the ER unit coordinator. The ER unit coordinator was not allowed to accept this if it was incomplete, and, if it was, the system would not allow the bed request to go forward. Any attempt to bypass using the system resulted in the house supervisor not processing the request and, ultimately, personally visiting with the "offending" physician. Adherence soared to 100% within one week.

Summary

The Six Sources of Influence helped us track that we were attending to all of the requisite actions of each category of change, at the individual, peer, and structural/organizational level. The six sources were so easy to remember and communicate with hospital staff about what we were doing and why, that we quickly gained their support.

Being clear about the culture change we wanted to effect and the actions we needed to take required time and persistence. It bears keeping in mind that this a years-long effort, not achievable within a few months or with a few projects.

The simplest way to conceptualize where to focus change in order to improve the culture of an organization is to frame it in terms of *changing behavior* to support the new environment you want, and *creating scientists* (learners) of all your staff. This requires as many blame-free learning opportunities as possible so that staff feel safe to experiment and learn from mistakes. This can take the form of workshops, sure, but it also takes the form of rewarding any attempts (like saying, "Thank you!") to incrementally improve the work environment, processes, quality, services, etc.

Changes also require attending to the Six Sources of Influence. We have to consider the personal motivation and the abilities of people to perform in the new culture. We have to harness the influence we have on each other while making it safe to learn, and we have to consider the structural aspects of the organization or environment in order to reinforce the right behaviors, and to prevent us from doing otherwise.

# Chapter 2 – Creating Alignment, Setting Priorities: The Architecture for Executives and Managers

## Structure

This chapter provides a structure for prioritizing strategic improvement, implementing daily management, measuring improvement progress, as well as monitoring accountability. The primary foci in this chapter are the roles and tools used by executives and managers. The next chapter will describe the roles and tools used by managers and their employees. Managers have the triple responsibilities of helping to set priorities, translating those priorities into operational terms, and then implementing them. Yes, they have the hardest job. Ironically, middle managers are usually the last to be included in these exercises. To their credit, my client hospitals fully involved senior and middle managers (and sometimes frontline managers in the smaller hospitals) in their strategic and operational planning discussions.

This structure reflects my work with a healthcare system that consisted of five hospitals. It evolved over time as we adjusted the forms and formats to meet the needs of each particular organization. The structure, models, and tools offered here are meant to provide a starting point for your unique journey. It is important to keep in mind that *all* of the structures, models, and tools are required at some point in order to make your journey a successful one.

The tools herein described reflect the first year's work for each level of leadership. As the primary facilitator of this structure for my client hospitals, I learned how to adjust the structure, methods, and approaches to meet their particular organizational needs.

Every hospital, organization, and department that uses these tools will naturally go through a learning curve. This is simply because these are new skills, and it takes practice and patience to get better at using them. Therefore, the structure, methods, and tools need to be adapted to fit your organization, culture, and experience. Simultaneously, by practicing adaptability, the organization *learns* to be adaptive. Remember that continuous learning and adaptability are primary skills in a Lean environment.

Many of the terms used are not clinical or hospital terms, per se. That was semi-intentional on my part. The hospital administrators wanted to break free from some of their thinking, so we adapted our language to include words not often used in hospitals. Getting heads wrapped around the idea of "No margin, no mission" was a major breakthrough, and it was a necessary one for people who thought "non-profit" meant not needing revenue to be equal to or greater than expenses. Hospitals are a business. So, we chose to adopt some of the terms used in business. That became very real for the administrators, when changes in legislation shrunk our profit margin from 13% to 3% and falling. This might not work for all hospital administrators, and different terms might work better. Again, adaptability is key.

The name of the hospital is fictitious because this is not about the hospital itself, but about the structural blueprint used. From an abstract perspective, the purpose of this blueprint is to provide vertical line of sight that appropriately engages all levels of the organization according to their role, skills, knowledge and expertise (Illustration 2.1).

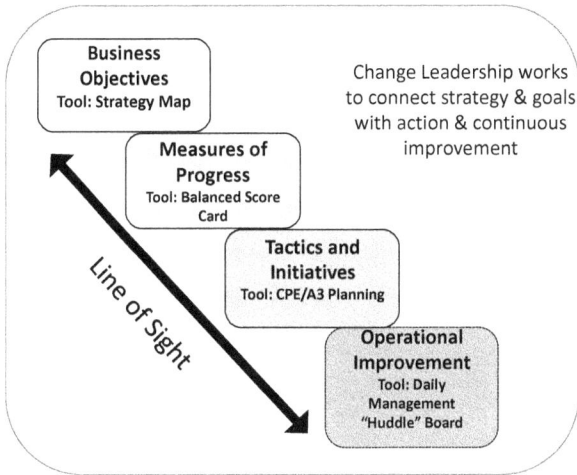

Illustration 2.1. Line of Sight.

Because the size of a hospital frequently determines the height of its hierarchy, and because we had five hospitals of different sizes, the number of meetings had to be scaled accordingly. Illustration 2.2 shows two different typical hierarchies within our system.

Regardless of "height of hierarchy," there are certain functions to which the different levels of leadership need to attend. Illustration 2.3 shows the different governing structures and roles that executive leaders, middle managers, frontline managers, and supervisors need to perform. Using an executive-level Balanced Scorecard to track the progress, top hospital leadership will need to define the strategies, measures, and objectives to focus and align the organization. Middle managers will then have to translate the strategic measures into daily operations. They must have a cross-departmental or cross-functional view of those operations to ensure the seamless integration of processes and services, using the Department Dashboard to monitor progress. Then, frontline managers and supervisors will turn those

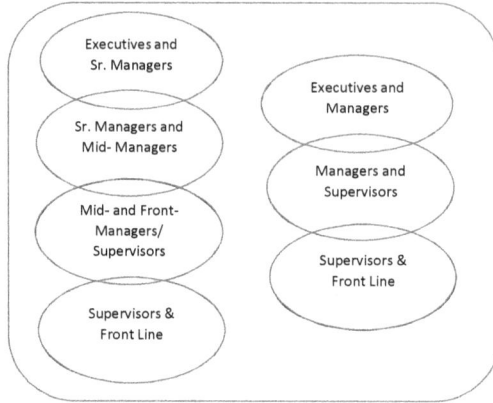

Illustration 2.2. Hospital Hierarchies.

objectives into staff-level measures and initiatives to supportively align their departments with the hospital improvement strategies.

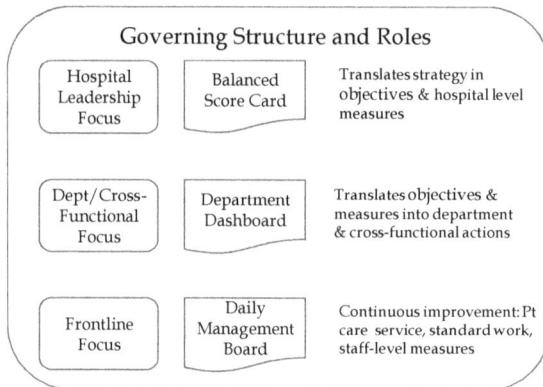

Illustration 2.3. Governing Structure and Roles.

Role of Executives and Senior Managers (CEOs, COOs, Presidents)

In addition to setting the direction for the organization, leaders define the market and also identify where major resources will be deployed. The main tools to use are the Strategy Map, Balanced

Scorecard and Initiatives Plan Matrix. For our purposes, these tools were combined into one structure as shown in Illustration 2.4. (The graphic is not legible at this size, but is presented here to show the whole framework.) The structure was printed on 3' x 5' paper and put on a wall so it was accessible in person and legible. This allowed us to see all our work at once, and allowed us to check for consistency, integration, and flow-down or cascade integrity. It also provided an immediate overview of the objectives, measures, initiatives, and projects that would align the hospital leadership and managers for the next year.

The result was that we could more easily convert the objectives into hospital-wide measures, initiatives, and Department Dashboards. Furthermore, we were able to identify areas of improvement and establish appropriate teams for high priority and/or cross-functional issues. The rest of this chapter will drill down into each aspect of this structure to show how they all fit together at the application level.

A hospital can start practically anywhere in the structure and be successful, but true, long-term sustainment will require all the elements to be present. As we were creating our structure, we referred to Pascal Dennis's and Jim Womack's approach described in *Getting the Right Things Done: A Leader's Guide to Planning and Execution*.[11] They use a series of A3s to accomplish much the same thing. In our case, we combined concepts and formats proffered by Robert S. Kaplan and David P. Norton, in addition to Pascal Dennis and Jim Womack. [12, 13] None is more "right" than the other; you simply have to make adjustments according to what works for your

---

[11] Dennis, Pascal and Jim Womack. *Getting the Right Things Done: A Leader's Guide to Planning and Execution*. Lean Enterprise Institute, 2006.

[12] Kaplan, Robert S. and David P. Norton. "The Balanced Scorecard: Measures that Drive Performance", *Harvard Business Review*. Jan–Feb 1992.

[13] Dennis, Pascal, "Strategy Deployment: What Is It? Why Should I Care?: Follow-up Q&A," *Lean Enterprise Institute*, 18 January, 2007, http://www.lean.org/post_strategy_deployment_webinar_qanda.html

organization's culture and style preference, as we did. That said, these tools typically work best when they are implemented at the leadership level, from where they will cascade down through all departments.

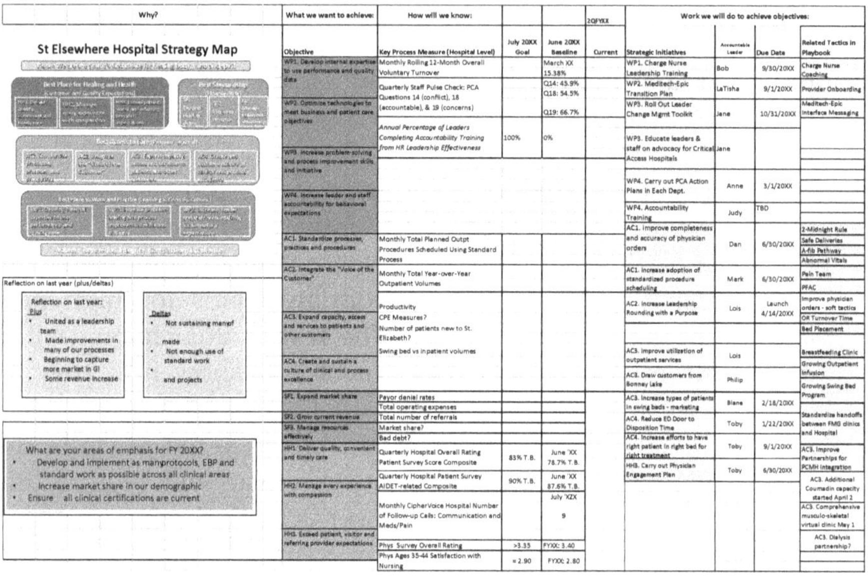

Illustration 2.4. Strategic Alignment and Priorities.

Regardless of structure, some form of hierarchal and level-appropriate measures are required to steer the organization. You likely already have some type of goal deployment mechanism in place. If something already exists, adjust that existing structure to align goals and measures to the format shown here. Then, align the measures to give the departments the ability to flow measures vertically down and horizontally across the organization.

Unfortunately, top level measures rarely have meaning to the frontline staff. This is where your managers will have to do the hard work of translating the top-level measures to simple and meaningful frontline measures in order for the frontline staff to carry them forward into action. For example, a strategic goal to increase revenue per patient will likely have to be translated into a measure at the RN level, such as how long it takes to do discharge plans.

Likewise, middle managers must translate up from frontline measures their relationship to the strategic measures. Illustration 2.5 provides two examples of this cascade and translation of executive strategic goals to frontline (MD, RN, Tech, Reg, and HUC), including possible projects or initiatives in which staff might engage to improve the process measures.

Notice that the measures and initiatives for both Registration (time to complete registration and improve registration process) and the Techs (time to complete vitals and standardizing vitals process) are the same across two different manager measures (both door to doc and doc to door). It is not unusual for one high-level measure to be supported by different initiatives, or for one initiative to support two or more higher-level measures.

Many goals are mandated from external sources, such as federal and state government or other regulatory entities. Incorporating all types of goals into the Strategy Map can be helpful, but not always possible. You cannot control everything, especially those things that are external. Using the strategy map structure is not meant to imply you can neatly put all issues and initiatives into one package, but it does organize some of the chaos.

| Strategy | Exectutive | Upper Manager | Manager | Staff | Initiative |
|---|---|---|---|---|---|
| Create and sustain clinical and process excellence | ED visits per Bed | Hours on Diversion | Doc to Admit | MD: Time from MD to Admit order | Reduce Time to Write Orders to <180' from Quick Reg. |
| | | | | RN: Time to Conduct Handoff | Standardize Handoff Instructions |
| | | | | Reg: Time to Complete Registration | Improve Registration Process to Integrate with Pt Care |
| | | | | Tech: Time to Complete Final Vitals | Standardize Final Vitals Process |

| Strategy | Executive | Upper Manager | Manager | Staff | Initiative |
|---|---|---|---|---|---|
| Create and sustain clinical and process excellence | Revenue per Patient | LWBS | Doc to Door | MD: Time to Write DC Orders | Reduce Time to Write Orders to <180' from Quick Reg. |
| | | | | RN: Time to Provide DC Instructions | Standardize DC Instructions |
| | | | | Reg: Time to Complete Registration | Improve Registration Process to Integrate with Pt Care |
| | | | | Tech: Time to Complete Final Vitals | Standardize Final Vitals Process |

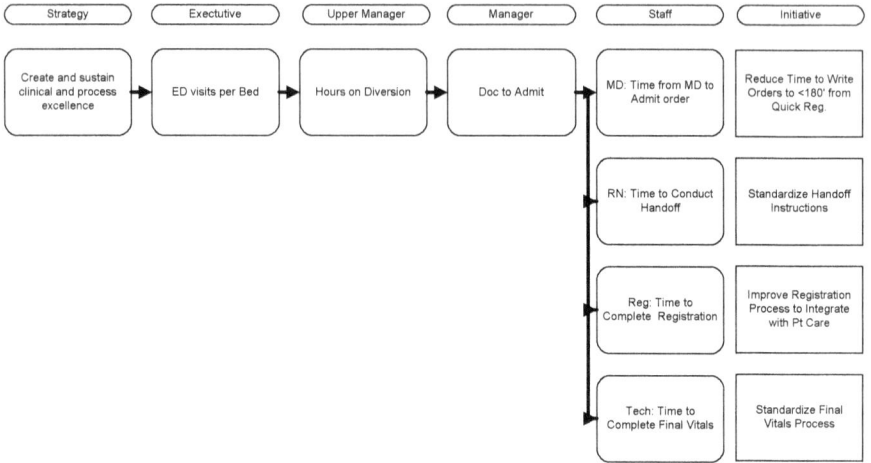

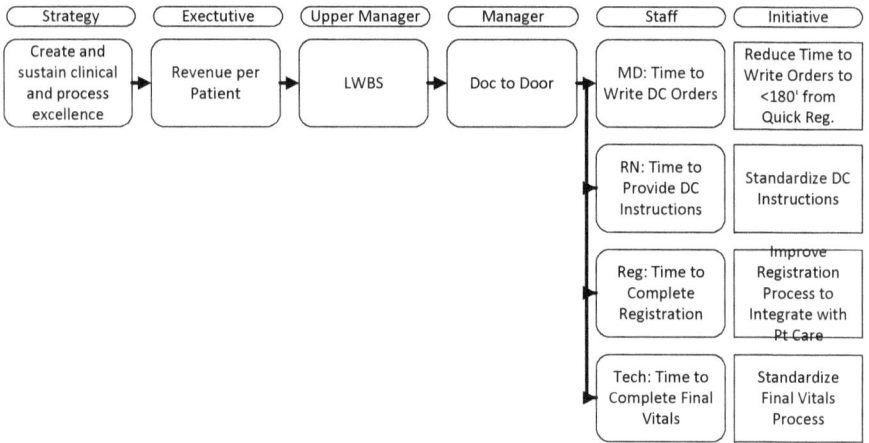

Illustration 2.5. Two Examples of Cascaded Measures.

44

Tools of Executives and Senior Managers

For leaders, the goals and measurements are those represented on the Strategy Map and Balanced Scorecard. These must be translated down to the organization, teams, and units. Likewise, leaders are informed upwards by mid-level and frontline-level translation of goals and measures. This allows them to determine what adjustments are necessary at the top in order to further improve guidance and cohesion down through the organization.

The description here is meant to show how to cascade the objectives from the executive Strategy Map, to your Balanced Scorecard, to middle management's Initiatives Plan to frontline activities. (This is discussed in detail in Chapter 3.)

The Strategy Map helps to make explicit what is most important to leadership, and helps to convey it to everyone in the organization.[14] Represented here is but one possible way to format the Strategy Map (Illustration 2.6). Google "strategy map" and you will discover hundreds of different designs. I started by giving my client a few examples of what other hospitals had done. Given those starting formats, my client was the primary driver in the adjustment of the look and feel of their map. This is the particular design that my client hospital settled on to best represent their work.

The particular alignment of the strategies as laid out in Illustration 2.6 is meant to show that these objectives and strategies are linked in a *causal relationship*, each layer dependent upon the success of the one below. To miss this causal relationship is to miss the value of a Strategy Map that separates it from merely categorizing your objectives. The causal relationship can be analyzed in reverse, or from top to bottom. To achieve Best Place for Healing and Health means that good processes need to be in place at the process/internal level (Best Access to Care). Good, effective

---

[14] Kaplan, Robert S. and David P. Norton. "Strategy Maps", *Harvard Business School Publishing Corporation*, 2004.

processes then need qualified and well-trained staff to execute them (Best Place to Work and Practice).

## Strategy Map

Vision: We are the Sound's first choice for healing

**Best Place for Healing and Health**
(Customer and Quality Expectations)

HH1. Deliver quality, convenient, timely, and safe care

HH2. Manage every experience with compassion and respect

HH3. Exceed patient, visitor and referring provider expectations

**Best Stewardship**
(Finance/Risk)

SF1. Expand market share south

SF2. Grow current revenue

SF3. Manage resources effectively

### Best Access to Care (Process/Internal)

AC1. Standardize processes, practices and procedures

AC2. Expand capacity, access and services to patients and referring providers

AC3. Integrate the Voice of our patients and families, staff, and providers

AC4. Partner with community stakeholders

### Best Place to Work and Practice (Learning & Growth, IT, Culture)

WP1. Recruit, develop, and retain awesome people – Competent Workforce

WP2. Create and sustain a culture of clinical and process excellence

WP3. Set expectations and hold teams accountable

WP4. Create a culture of Engagement

Values: Reverence, Integrity, Compassion, Excellence

Illustration 2.6. St Elsewhere Hospital Strategy Map.

For example, let's say that the ED has a goal for stroke patients to receive treatment within 30 minutes of arrival to the hospital. This would be under objective HH1: "Deliver quality, convenient, and timely care." To achieve this 30-minute goal might require using Lean workshops to improve the process and standardize the work until it can be performed seamlessly again and again at the target rate. Of course, the doctors, nurses, and techs performing diagnoses and treatments for the patient would participate in the improvement work.

The different shades in the Strategy Map also represent an important concept of strategy development and measurement: a balance across the different aspects of the business. While it is typical for organizations to be focused on the financial measures of success (Finance/Risk), we must be careful not to sacrifice other aspects of the business that must also be developed and improved. That is, we must develop the people who provide the service (Learning & Growth). We must improve the processes by which care is given (Process/Internal), and we must improve the patient experience of our care (Customer and Quality Expectations).

Oftentimes this leveling results in what is known as a Balanced Scorecard. Kaplan and Norton describe in great detail the value and mechanics of creating different types of Balanced Scorecards, and I recommend reading their material.[14]

We represented the Balanced Scorecard approach within the Objectives Matrix by using the colors to designate which area of the strategy map it referenced (Illustration in 2.7). The strategies were given alphanumeric designations to make for easier cross-referencing between the Strategy Map and the Objectives Matrix. In turn, the strategies provided greater specificity as to how this hospital wanted to attain each particular objective.

In Illustration 2.7, under the columns titled, "What we want to achieve," and "How will we know," we articulated more clearly our objectives by developing yardsticks by which we would measure progress. This is a critical element of achieving strategic objectives. It does no good to state, "We want to be number one," if we don't know what that means or whether we are progressing toward that goal. Could you imagine a sports team winning the championship if they didn't measure each athlete's performance or how the team cooperates on the field for each game?

A distinction needs to be made, though, between a measure and a goal. These are very frequently confused. A measure does not say in which direction you want to go. It does not say improve, reduce, increase, fastest, biggest, etc. It simply states what will be measured and the unit of measure. The goal states the direction. For example,

---

[14] Kaplan, Robert S. and David P. Norton. "The Balanced Scorecard: Translating Strategy into Action." *Harvard Business School Press*. 1996.

if our goal is to beat our time at running the mile, then we need to measure distance, time, and speed. To that we add direction and it becomes a fully stated goal: to run a mile in 8 minutes, with a baseline of 10 minutes, as of spring season 2014.

Each objective may need one or more measures and goals. I recommend keeping in mind two things when identifying measures and goals. First, you are looking for indicators of success, so too low of a level or too fine a detail may likely not be beneficial. For example, at this level we want to measure overall hospital acquired conditions (HACs), not how many hospital acquired infections (HAIs) the Med/Surg department had. Second, having too many measures and goals makes it harder to keep everyone focused on the right things. Leaders, managers and staff will begin to pick and choose for themselves what to achieve if there are too many alternatives.

| What we want to achieve: | How will we know: | | | 2QFYXX |
|---|---|---|---|---|
| | | July 20XX Goal | June 20XX Baseline | |
| Objective | Key Process Measure (Hospital Level) | July 20XX Goal | June 20XX Baseline | Current |
| WP1. Develop internal expertise to use performance and quality data | Monthly Rolling 12-Month Overall Voluntary Turnover | | 50/234 | |
| | | | 15.38% | |
| | Quarterly Staff Pulse Check: PCA | | Q14: 45.9% | |
| WP2. Increase problem-solving and process improvement skills and initiative | Questions 14 (conflict), 18 (accountable), & 19 (concerns) | | Q19: 66.7% | |
| WP3. Increase leader and staff accountability for behavioral expectations | Annual Percentage of Leaders Completing Accountability Training from HR Leadership Effectiveness | 100% | 0% | |
| AC1. Standardize processes, practices and procedures | Monthly Total Planned Output Procedures Scheduled Using Standard Process | | | |
| AC2. Integrate the "Voice of the Customer" | Monthly Total Year-over-Year Outpatient Volumes | | | |
| AC3. Expand capacity, access and services to patients and other customers | Number of patients new to St. Elsewhere | | | |
| AC4. Create and sustain a culture of clinical and process excellence | ED Door to Dispo and Dispo to Discharge/Admit | | | |
| | Reduce unnecessary transfers of Pts | | | |
| SF1. Expand market share | Total number of referrals | | | |
| SF2. Grow current revenue | Payor denial rates | | | |
| SF3. Manage resources effectively | Total operating expenses | | | |
| HH1. Deliver quality, convenient and timely care | Quarterly Hospital Overall Rating Patient Survey Score Composite | 83% T.B. | June 20XX 78.7% T.B. | |
| HH2. Manage every experience with compassion | Quarterly Hospital Patient Survey AIDET-related Composite | 90% T.B. | June 20XX 87.6% T.B. | |
| HH3. Exceed patient, visitor and referring provider expectations | Monthly CipherVoice Hospital Number of Follow-up Calls: Communication | >3.35 | FYXX: 3.40 | |
| | Phys Survey Overall Rating | = 2.90 | FYXX: 2.80 | |
| | Phys Ages 35-44 Satisfaction with Nursing | | | |

Illustration 2.7. St Elsewhere Objectives Matrix.

The importance of the Plus/Delta comparison, shown in Illustration 2.8, is that it provides a narrative of how leadership believes the organization performed. Upon reflection of the last year, it informs leadership about adjustments they'll need to make next year.

| Reflections on last year: | |
|---|---|
| Pluses | Deltas |
| *United as leadership team | *Not sustaining all improvements |
| *Improved many processes | *Not enough use of standard work |
| *Capturing more GI market | *Still too many projects |
| *Some ED revenue increase | |

Illustration 2.8. Plus/Deltas.

Then, combining how we did last year with our strategies and objectives for the next year, we can articulate the areas of emphasis for the next year (Illustration 2.9). This does not replace the strategies or objectives, but adds an underlying theme or context to help guide decisions and activities.

| **What are your are of emphasis for FY 20XX?** |
|---|
| **\*Develop and implement as many protocols, EBP, and standard work as possible across all clinical area** |
| **\*Increase market share in our demographic;** |
| **\*Ensure all clinical  certifications are current** |

Illustration 2.9 Emphasis Areas.

The Initiatives Plan shown in Illustration 2.10 is one of the most important steps, and needs time and patience to implement and maintain. The matrix is used to show the relationship between the actions and their respective objectives and measures. This is the "work we will do to achieve objectives."

It is not necessary to list the same action more than once, even if the action affects more than one objective. Usually, the action is listed on the same line as its strongest relationship. In every organization of which I have been a part, everyone has been tasked with doing too many projects. Those responsible for the projects often didn't understand how these projects supported the organization's strategies, goals and objectives. This matrix is designed to help make those connections.

| | | | |
|---|---|---|---|
| **Work we will do to achieve objectives:** | | | |
| **Initiatives** | **Accountable Leader** | **Due Date** | **Related Tactics** |
| WP1. Charge Nurse Leadership Training | Bob | 9/30/20XX | Charge Nurse Coaching |
| WP2. Educate leaders & staff on advocacy for Critical Access Hospitals | LaTisha | 9/1/20XX | Provider Onboarding |
| WP3. Carry out PCA Plans in Each Dept. | Jane | 10/31/20XX | |
| WP3. Accountability | Jane | 3/1/20XX | |
| AC1. Increase adoption of standardized procedure scheduling | Anna | TBD | 2-Midnight Rule |
| | | | Safe Deliveries |
| | | | A-fib Pathway |
| AC2. Increase Leadership Rounding with a Purpose | Judy | 6/30/20XX | Pain Team |
| | | | PFAC |
| AC3. Increase types of patients in swing beds - marketing | Dan | nch 4/14/20XX | Grow Swing Bed Program |
| AC4. Reduce ED Door to Disposition Time | Mark | 6/30/20XX | First time to quality (FTQ) |
| | | | Bed Placement |
| AC4. Improve Pt placement: right patient in right bed for right treatment | Lois | 6/30/20XX | Breastfeeding Clinic |
| | | | Growing Outpatient infusion |
| SF1. Improve referral rate from Med Group | Philip | 6/30/20XX | |
| SF2. Improve coding of procedures | Hanna | 6/30/20XX | |
| SF3. Teach managers productivity tools and systems | Blaine | 6/30/20XX | |
| HH1. Implement quick rounds | Toby | 1/22/20XX | |
| HH2. Implement AIDET | Toby | 9/1/20XX | AIDET |
| HH3. Carry out Physician Engagement Plan | Toby | 9/1/20XX | |

Illustration 2.10. St Elsewhere Initiatives Plan.

Though Illustration 2.10 reflects the completion of the matrix, the actual rendering of the initiatives list took a different form. The purpose is to narrow down activities to those which best leverage your resources of people, time and money. There is a good chance your staff are getting burned out from having too many projects, initiatives, or activities. They want to do a few things well, rather than many things poorly.

If done well, this step frequently results in the reduction of the number of these projects, initiatives, and activities by 40-50%, easily. This step takes time, courage, and willingness to keep revisiting the goals and needs for each project. This is your chance to really ask the hard questions about the value of your enterprise. These are samples of the questions we asked for every project, initiative and activity:

- Which strategy (and/or the objectives and goals) does this specific project help us to accomplish?
- How does this project actually help us "move the dial" and truly meet our objectives?
- How strong is the relationship between project and strategy? In other words, does this project really make a difference in meeting that strategy, or is it a minor player?
- Are there any strategies or objectives that are not supported or are under-supported by the project, initiative, or activity?
- If yes, are they important enough to be supported by definitive action? Is it necessary to add further initiatives to the list?

Tip: On the question of "strength" of relationship, some departments found it useful to create a separate matrix. They listed each initiative on the left column, and then listed along the top of the next three columns the following criteria by which to judge the value of each activity by several important indices:

- Impact on resources, such as time, dollars, etc.
- True commitment
- Emotional investment

After narrowing the list of activities, they identified specific people with specific deadlines. Each activity leader was required to develop an action plan to achieve their objective. The action plans and progress were discussed in weekly leadership meetings.

The last column in the matrix, "Related Tactics," was our catch-all for such things as nationally-led activities and initiatives over which we had no control but that affected us nonetheless; other hospitals or hospital systems that were doing activities that impacted us; or emerging ideas that may have become separate initiatives of their own. Again, it is all a work in progress.

It is important to note, too, that creating the elements of this matrix took several hours over several sessions, and was accomplished by a team consisting of the hospital president, associate vice-presidents, directors, and managers.

Role of Senior and Middle Managers (Associate Vice-Presidents, Directors, Clinical Managers)

Tasked with ensuring their departments are performing well, the managers of managers also examine organizational processes for connection issues across departments, functions, and service lines. Theirs is a big-picture, operational worldview. They start with the Initiatives Plan, as seen above in Illustration 2.10, and then link them to the Department Dashboard's measures. These managers convert strategies into hospital-wide, departmental, or cross-functional initiatives and measures. It is at this level, then, where operational deployment and improvement turn those strategies into reality. Further responsibilities of this level of managers are:

- To take action on strategic goals and measures in order to ensure effective actions and countermeasures.
- To ensure continuous improvement meetings occur and are effective for solving departmental problems.
- To ensure cross-functional teams are assembled to address cross-functional and high-priority issues.

- To facilitate improvement and problem-solving conversation as appropriate. The role of the experienced, facilitative manager is to help staff to help themselves improve.
- To coach frontline managers and ensure that:
  - o Effective problem solving is occurring in teams.
  - o The daily management system is effectively getting results connected to customer and business requirements.
  - o Work priorities are clear to frontline managers.

Tools of Senior and Middle Managers

Clinical departments have a multitude of measures, usually on Department Dashboards. Department Dashboards are used to identify and prioritize the measures that will be actively managed and cascaded to frontline based upon the strategic prerogatives of hospital leadership. Illustration 2.11 is an example of a simplified Department Dashboard from an emergency department.

| Measure | Target minutes | April 2018 | | April 2019 | | May 2018 | | May 2019 | | June 2018 | | June 2019* | |
|---|---|---|---|---|---|---|---|---|---|---|---|---|---|
| ED Volume | | | 3924 | | 4150 | | 4158 | | 4234 | | 3938 | | 4143 |
| LWOBS | 1.50% | 2.09% | 82 | 1.10% | 48 | 1.92% | 80 | 0.80% | 37 | 3.83% | 151 | 1.60% | 66 |
| AMA | | | 22 | | 54 | | 12 | | 45 | | 39 | | 52 |
| LOS Admitted | 299 | 372 | 751 | 381 | 807 | 324 | 730 | 359 | 813 | 373 | 603 | 346 | 803 |
| LOS Discharged | 157 | 194 | 3138 | 201 | 3100 | 177 | 3361 | 190 | 3185 | 202 | 2848 | 243 | 3129 |
| LOS Transferred | | 488 | 34 | 284 | 45 | 723 | 67 | 351 | 47 | 345 | 35 | 495 | 45 |
| Door to Provider | 30 | 44.7 | | 28.23 | | 36.8 | | 21.15 | | 74.88 | | 26 | |
| Door to Bed | 7 | 22.7 | | 16.63 | | 20.1 | | 12.12 | | 38 | | 16 | |
| Boarder to Floor | 30 | 151.5 | | 102 | | 129.5 | | 84.5 | | 103 | | 97 | |
| Arrive to Decis | 112 | 149.4 | | 248 | | 149 | | 236 | | 259 | | 248 | |

Illustration 2.11 ED Department Dashboard.

The mid-level measures allow managers to effectively organize the department. However, as one manager put it, "we are data rich and information poor. There exists more data than we could possibly use or monitor." The challenge is to align existing measures with strategic goals, not at the exclusion of required clinical measures, but in order to focus attention on the high-leverage goals and measures that give the best indication of the performance of the department in its service to patients.

How do our actions contribute to the organization's direction, goals and objectives? The manager is responsible for looking across departments and functions for interface, handoff, and cross-functional issues that impede good flow of patient care. Measures should reflect this perspective. What is your measure for patient throughput or test result turnaround? The Department Dashboard should reflect the translation of leadership or executive measures to the managerial level, while also being a springboard for the frontline measures. Illustration 2.11 provides two examples of this cascade and translation. To engage frontline staff with improving the measure and goals appropriate at their level, a manager will need to select the most appropriate measures for managing her unit.

Another tool for mid-managers is the Manager Visual Control standard work (Illustration 2.12). This standard work is used by mid-managers to track unit progress alongside department goals and objectives, as reflected on unit Visual Controls or Daily Management Boards. Daily Management Boards are discussed at length in Chapter 3.

| Strategy | Exectutive | Manager | Staff | Initiative |
|---|---|---|---|---|
| Create and sustain clinical and process excellence | Revenue per Patient | Avg LOS in ED | MD: Door to Doc | Reduce Time to See New Patients |
| | | | RN: Time to Triage | Standardize Triage Process |
| | | | Reg: Time to do Quick Registration | Standardize Quick Reg. Process |
| | | | Tech: Time to escort Pt to Bed | Standardize Communication Process to Techs |

| Strategy | Exectutive | Manager | Staff | Initiative |
|---|---|---|---|---|
| Create and sustain clinical and process excellence | LWBS | LWBS | MD: Door to Doc | Reduce Time to See New Patients |
| | | | RN: Time to Triage | Standardize Triage Process |
| | | | Reg: Time to do Quick Registration | Standardize Quick Reg. Process |
| | | | Tech: Time to escort Pt to Bed | Standardize Communication Process to Techs |

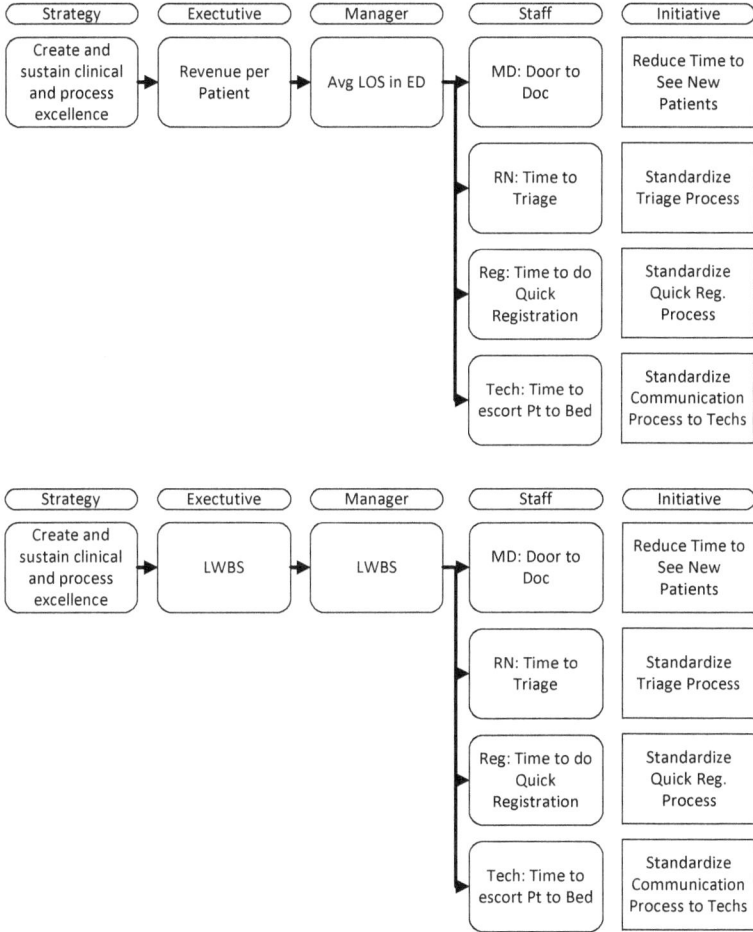

Illustration 2.12. Example of Cascaded Measures.

| Manager Visual Controls | |
|---|---|
| Date:<br><br>Department:<br><br> | |
| Intent | Visual Controls should do at least three things:<br>• Reflect the actual vs. expected performance, pace or progression of work<br>• Capture cause analysis on delays, interruptions, and frustrations that arise doing the work<br>• Reflect the impact of actions taken to improve performance |
| **Diagnostic Questions - Is there evidence that:** | |
| The right things are measured (for the right reason)? | Yes/No |
| There are visual tracking charts in the area? | Yes/No |
| The charts are current? | Yes/No |
| The visual tracking charts clearly and dramatically shows actual versus expected (target) performance? | Yes/No |
| The charts clearly and easily tell if performance is improving or not? | Yes/No |
| There is gap analysis (root cause analysis) being done that describes a gap in performance? | Yes/No |
| There are countermeasures, plans, process improvements (corrective actions) to bridge the gap(s)? | Yes/No |
| The countermeasures are clear, specific, and actionable? | Yes/No |
| Assignments are given for corrective actions (countermeasures/plans/process improvement)? | Yes/No |
| The impact of countermeasures are reflected in the visual controls for outcomes/results/progress? | Yes/No |
| Leaders review the visual controls/performance indicators on a regular and consistent basis? | Yes/No |
| Managers are *using* the visual controls/charts to manage the work? | Yes/No |
| Staff are *using* the visual controls/charts to do the work? | Yes/No |
| Leaders review the visuals/performance with suppliers and/or customers (internal or external) on a regular and consistent basis? | Yes/No |
| Reviews with suppliers and/or customers (other functions) result in action? | Yes/No |
| Charts are revised, added and dropped as things change? | Yes/No |
| Visual charts are regularly used not only by "operations" but by support staff in the division? (If applicable) | Yes/No |

Illustration 2.13. Manager Standard Work for Visual Controls.

Role of Middle to Frontline Managers

The middle and frontline managers' combined view of the world is tactical and operational. The role of the middle to frontline managers is to:

- Adhere to manager standard work and use standard Lean problem-solving tools.
- Check work processes.
- Check staff adherence to standard work.
- Coach staff and ask questions to ensure effective problem solving is occurring in teams daily.
- Ensure cross-functional improvements are implemented, staff are trained, and results are visible.
- Ensure Daily Management Board is used to:
    o Plan and lead weekly continuous improvement meetings using DMB.
    o Update boards, lead huddles, and follow standard agenda.
    o Connect the levels of daily work and ensure there is a plan for meeting customer and business requirements.
    o Develop and maintain relevant measures that quickly tell the units how they are performing their daily work (actual measure) against the level of performance you want to achieve (target measure).
    o Ensure countermeasures are taken when targets are not met.
    o Ensure work priorities are clear and visible for staff.

## Tools of Middle to Frontline Managers

The main tools to use will be the standard work and Daily Management Board. Descriptions of the roles and tools of frontline managers, supervisors, and staff, and how they contribute to the strategic goals by focusing on operational improvements, is provided in greater detail in Chapter 3.

## The Strategic to Operational Structure is in Place. Now what?!

I could have easily put this discussion at the end of Chapter 3, which is the detailed frontline activity, but it belongs here because of the focus of this chapter on the action of leaders after the strategic planning is done.

My experience in the past has been that strategic planning ends at the moment the leaders agree on the strategy. Then it goes on the shelf. Sometimes, the role of leaders is passive in relation to the very goals they have set out to achieve. For most leaders today, the typical scenario is that senior leadership invites managers to meetings so they can answer questions and give updates. As a leader, you hope the information you're being given is not filtered to make other leaders look good or to not look as bad.

There are actions you can take to better understand how well your goals and plans are being accomplished. In Lean, the best practice for senior leadership is to go directly to where the work gets done. Operational rounding at the department level is a must for transitioning an organization into embracing the Lean culture. Operational rounding (akin to patient rounding) means looking at the operational measures and action plans at the *gemba*. A Japanese word meaning the "actual place" or "real place," in Lean culture, *gemba* describes a deeper awareness of the actual workplace, of seeing the actual process, and talking to staff at every level. In this scenario, you might go talk to frontline staff to determine how effectively your strategy is being cascaded into operations, and to personally see how well your managers and frontline staff are improving quality and service delivery.

Use your time at the *gemba* to:

- Visit the Daily Management Boards.
- Observe huddles—both operational and clinical.
- Check manager and staff adherence to standard work.
- Coach managers and observe progress to ensure target and process measures are in place.
- Ensure strategic efforts and objectives have been translated to the frontline.

In other words, do staff know what is expected of them? Do they have the capacity and capability to support strategic objectives?

An example of this type of conversation occurred in a hospital when the leader went to the *gemba* to ask staff how the door-to-doc time (D2D) could be reduced to less than 30 minutes. Frontline stated that they could achieve faster D2D time if staff schedules were changed and if there could be minor remodeling. The leader addressed the scheduling and found the money to do some minor remodeling at the entrance to the Emergency Department to facilitate moving patients through triage. The ED team was able to meet the executive's objective of D2D time of less than 30 minutes. In the previous administration, leaders had the same expectation for the ED to meet the D2D time within 30 minutes; however, the ED's logistical ability to actually accomplish the target was not possible. It caused great embarrassment to the hospital when the ED could not meet the marketed 30-minute goal.

The point is, if a leader wants to be in touch with operations, the leader needs to go *directly* to operations. Depending on the size of the hospital and the number of patients, this operational rounding should be no less than quarterly to each department, and as frequently as weekly.

One administrator made it a habit of periodically going to the daily huddles and dashboards to encourage and cheerlead everyone, and to see if the operational alignment between frontline and strategy was happening. When it wasn't, the administrator would have a follow-up conversation with that group's managers to help coach them on alignment issues.

Plainly said, this is not a "dog and pony" show put on for the leader, but an operational meeting among the executives and staff to see how things are *really* going. If it is a surprise that you are visiting or is somehow something *special*, then you are likely not visiting enough. And, just as importantly, if you are not visiting the *gemba* frequently enough, real alignment to hospital goals and objectives is likely not happening.

Summary

We covered the activities and formats that you can use to create, cascade, and translate high-level strategies into operational objectives, initiatives and activities that managers and frontline will implement to achieve those strategies. We encourage you to engage each successive level in the planning activity as your organization moves down the ladder. In other words, there should always be an overlap between each vertical level in the organization so that less is lost in translation.

While the specific tools and formats are not as important, the imperative is to address each aspect of a balanced and interdependent strategy, measured by balanced indicators that reduce the tendency to focus too much on any one aspect of the business. Each level of the organization will likely use some variation or derivation of the tools and formats used by the next higher level. They might also use different tools, like the Daily Management Board, versus a Strategic Plan, to monitor progress and improve operations in the direction you, as leaders, have set.

Finally, confirming compliance with the strategic objectives is best done in person. These visits are not meant to be hunts and "gotcha" moments, but rather a sincere effort to help those who actually provide patient care with the support they need to accomplish your mission. This might mean removing roadblocks or solving problems only your authority can provide.

# Chapter 3 – Frontline Focus: The Architecture for Managers, Supervisors and Employees

## Making a Difference

Everyone wants to make a difference and know that what they do contributes to something greater than themselves. If employees are engaged in their work, they are more likely to provide better care and better services to patients. Engagement, though, is more than just providing team activities. Employees also want to be respected by their supervisors and co-workers for their knowledge and abilities. Engaged employees contribute more to an organization's mission than do daily tasks. Employees take pride in workplace because they want theirs to be the best. Who doesn't want to be part of a winning team?

So what does it take to truly engage staff in improving the performance of the unit, and, ultimately, the organization? It is important to consider that the frontline view of the world is tactical and operational. The strategies that were developed by leaders will have little meaning to staff unless it is put in such terms. Engaging staff begins with translating the strategic view into daily activities performed by frontline staff. But while frontline staff are immersed in the process, they may not see holistically the process they are steeped in. They know the tasks that they have to complete every day, but rarely see the upstream and downstream effects of those actions—what we call a "heads-down" perspective. However, if they look at and map the whole process, they are quite adept at helping to make improvements to it. They perform the work every day, and therefore have the best knowledge and perspective on how to improve the process.

The challenge, however, is for middle managers—usually with the help of a Lean advisor—to help staff connect the dots of the individual activities (getting supplies, assigning patients, obtaining medicine, discharging, etc.) to the larger process in order to understand the upstream and downstream impact of their actions. Middle managers also need to align the daily work of staff to larger process and organizational goals. The key is to make this obvious to staff so everyone is on the same page.

Strategic planning is a "heads-up" perspective. Many of the tools of Lean, such as process mapping, begin to give frontline staff that bigger picture perspective.

An example of this was the tendency for Med/Surg nurses to hold homeless patients until lunch time. They wanted the patient to have another meal before being discharged. As you can imagine, this extra time was costly to the hospital. In addition, this procedure had the unintended consequence of increasing holds in the Emergency Department because patients could not be brought up to the unit. When we pointed this out to the nurses, they solved the problem by ordering lunches in a box that the patient could take with them, and so they could be discharged earlier. This had a significant impact on both the ED and Med/Surg.

As shown in Illustration 3.1, the four methods or mechanisms for engaging frontline staff consist of 1) the Daily Management Board;

2) huddles; 3) improvement teams; and 4) standard work. They each serve their own purpose and are used to augment each other.

In short, the **Daily Management Board** provides performance information to track improvements and outcomes so that appropriate action can be taken to resolve current problems and prevent future problems. DMBs are also necessary to see the impact that new initiatives are having.

**Shift huddles** engage staff by asking them to bring problems and ideas forward for making those improvements. Huddles are an opportunity for staff to participate in daily problem solving, to follow through on assigned action items, and to help the team measure success of improvements.

**Improvement teams** can take multiple forms, from multi-day workshops to assigning a project to a group of staff in order to solve a problem or improve a process. The main objective with improvement teams is to assemble a group of people affected by the issue who can work collaboratively to fix it.

A key tenet of Lean is standardizing and stabilizing processes. **Standard work** is one of the most valuable tools for achieving a stable process. So, the output of almost all activities, whether they are workshops, 5S, huddles, or otherwise, should be standard work.

Let's look at each of these in further detail below.

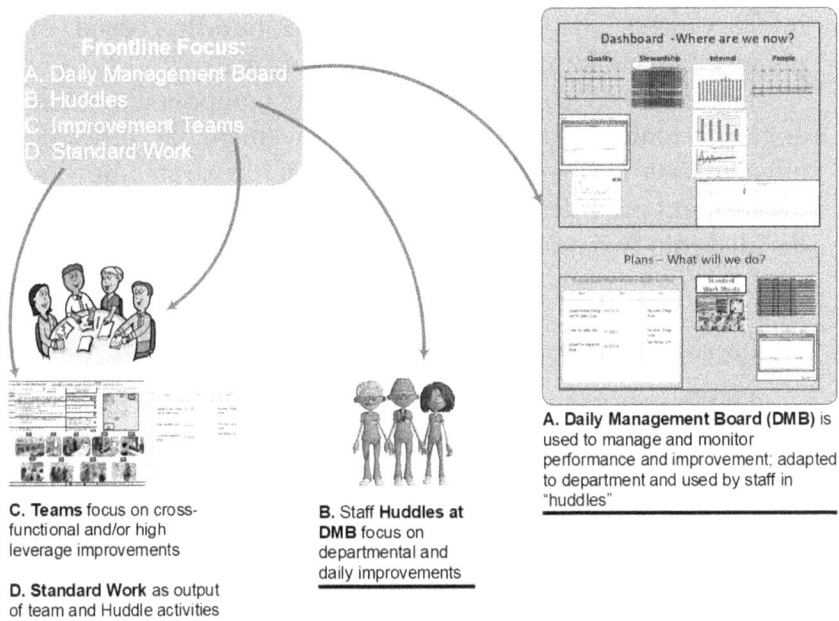

A. **Daily Management Board (DMB)** is used to manage and monitor performance and improvement; adapted to department and used by staff in "huddles"

C. **Teams** focus on cross-functional and/or high leverage improvements

D. **Standard Work** as output of team and Huddle activities

B. Staff **Huddles** at **DMB** focus on departmental and daily improvements

Illustration 3.1. Frontline Focus.

Section A: Daily Management Board

The purpose of the Daily Management Board, shown also in Illustration 3.2, is to provide a means to display, monitor and manage the priorities of leadership and the department or unit. If deployed well, the Daily Management Board (DMB), used in conjunction with huddles, is one of the most powerful tools a manager can use to engage employees in improving the quality, financial health, and operations. It is an asset to increasing the professional development of employees.

There is a common misperception that Lean and process improvement is the purview of frontline. While it is frontline employees that have the daily knowledge and experience to improve the work they do, it is the manager's obligation to lead these discussions and to inform staff about possibilities and constraints of

67

improvements discussed at the DMB huddle, based on their perspective and knowledge of the organization.

The DMB is comprised of several components intended to engage frontline staff in the improvement of efficiency and effectiveness by displaying data that demonstrates how well the department provides patient care. The Daily Management Board is divided into two sections: the "Dashboard" and "Plans."

Dashboard — Where Are We Now?

The Dashboard reflects the priorities of the department. Similar to a Balanced Scorecard used by leadership, the measures can be grouped into the four typical categories: customer/quality, stewardship/financial, internal/process, and people/employees.

The Balanced Scorecard approach, replicated here as a Dashboard, is intended to remind us of the balance of factors that constitute a more complete picture of the health of the organization. We must not get too narrowly focused on one type of measure, and must be cautious of unintentionally and adversely affecting other measures. For example, too much emphasis on reducing costs might result in the lack of necessary equipment for staff to provide good patient care; we don't want to sacrifice quality care for faster care.

I have found that it is important to be flexible and adaptable about having measures for each category. Let the measures evolve as they prove their value to the work group and unit.

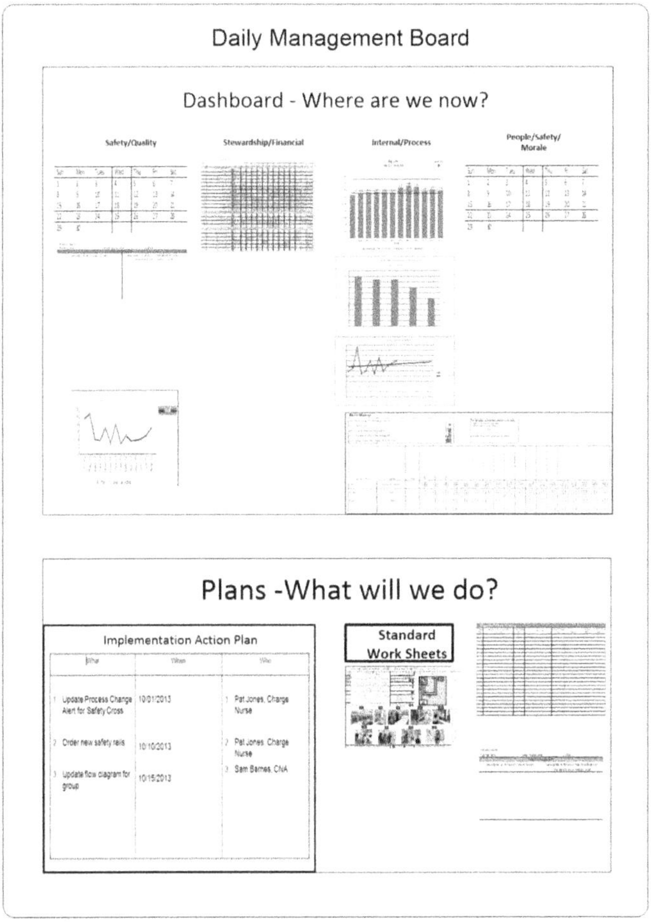

Illustration 3.2. Daily Management Board Example.

General Note About Measures

For managers and frontline staff, identifying the true indicators of performance and knowing where to investigate further are essential skills. We will need process measures that indicate predictable, consistent means of achieving safety and quality measures. Unfortunately, most measures tend to become outcome measures, and are not immediately available until weeks, months, or even quarters later.

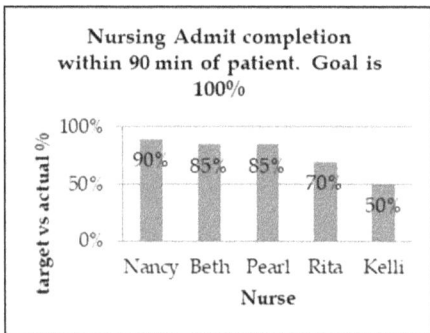

**Nursing Admit completion within 90 min of patient. Goal is 100%**

| Admit completion within 90 min. of Pt arriving on unit. Goal is 100% | |
|---|---|
| Nancy | 90% |
| Beth | 85% |
| Pearl | 85% |
| Rita | 70% |
| Kelli | 50% |

Illustration 3.3. Example of Data Presented in Graph Versus Table.

Measures can be represented by charts, graphs or tables — anything that easily shows the progress the department is making toward achieving its goals. Trend charts tend to work best for showing the direction of progress. We are visual beings, so a graph is usually more immediately understandable than a table or matrix. It's also important to include targets or goals that clearly show the difference between where you actually are and where you want to be. This visible difference is the performance gap that needs to be closed. That is the work of the improvement team during the huddles and workshops. Illustration 3.3 provides an example of how we can visualize much more quickly and easily the performance of the nurses. Sometimes a visual cue makes all the difference.

Having clear measures and goals are essential to achieving organizational success. Without them, staff does not acquire a line-of-sight commitment to strategic objectives. Since most measures and goals are developed and available at the management level, they must be cascaded to the frontline. This is not always easy to do. One reason it is not easy to transfer manager measures to frontline measures is that managers and leaders are so accustomed to their particular measures, and these measures are not always understood and actionable by everyone in the organization.

In fact, very few management measures are actionable at the frontline level as they are stated. For example, one common measure for a unit is Average Length of Stay (ALOS). There are few nurses who will know how to directly impact ALOS, per se, unless this measure is broken down into discreet units, such as time taken to admit or discharge a patient. Another example is Door to Doc time. Frontline can affect this measure at the individual level by tracking and reducing the time taken to register and triage patients, as well as the length of time needed to get the patient to a bed. Because this is the level on which the frontline works, not at the aggregate Door to Doc level, individual efforts greatly affect the larger measures.

If readmissions have been a problem, especially with not being reimbursed for 30-day readmits, then this management measure might be useful to have on the Dashboard, along with completion of a discharge checklist to ensure patients are properly prepared to go home.

One way to know if the measure has been transferred to the frontline is when a manager can assign a staff member's name to the measure. For example, Registrar Sally typically takes five minutes to register patients, whereas Bob takes ten minutes. By having their names next to the performance measure on a trend chart, we can challenge staff to achieve higher levels of performance and hold them accountable for doing so in the context of improving the processes and systems by which they do their work.

Whether you *should* put their name by the measure depends on your organization's culture and the trust staff have among themselves to not feel blamed but, rather, challenged. Some groups like a bit of friendly competition, and this can be a great way to spur that on. However, if your organization tends toward negative attribution, initially you might leave the names off.

Each department must identify these measures for themselves. Adjust as you learn from their use. Select measures that are actionable by the staff. Remember, staff cannot do anything about length of stay, but they can perform timely admits. If you choose to scale up your measures, rather than put them on the Daily Management Board all at once, then the focus should be first on patient and staff safety, then quality of service and timeliness of delivery, and focused lastly, then, on cost.

The importance of identifying process-level measures as soon as possible, especially those that can provide near to instant feedback, cannot be overstated. While management-level measures are necessary, they usually cannot be obtained more frequently than a week at best, but usually on a monthly basis. This is likely too slow for your organization to know if the changes are having an impact. Ideally, process-level measures will be available at the same time the action is being taken, and no later than 24 hours. This will enable the team to receive the information needed to promptly adjust their countermeasures.

One team consisting of Critical Care and Emergency Department nurses found the measures to be critical in clarifying fact from fiction. They believed that a major cause of delay in being able to move patients from the Emergency Department to the inpatient floors was that the hospital beds were not turned over and available quickly enough for the next patient. After counting instances in which the beds were not ready for the admitting patient, they discovered that rarely was the bed actually unprepared. Instead, they found that the more frequent occurrence was that the ED nurse was not able to locate a Critical Care nurse to whom to give the verbal report. They called this "myth busting." They soon became obsessed with determining reality from myths, realizing that only by knowing what is really happening could they fix it. Only data could negate the stories they had told themselves through the years. As the saying goes, "In God we trust. All others bring data!"

<u>Root Cause Analysis</u>

In discussing measures, we are looking for any incidents or trends that indicate either a problem or a lack of progress toward an improved state. Ask yourselves, "what does this graph tell us about any problems or process issues we are experiencing?" Then, use a root cause analysis method, such as the "5 Whys." The assumption here is that we are seeing the symptoms of an underlying cause that needs to be identified. Much like a medical diagnosis, we assume the symptom belies a deeper cause. The same is true for operational issues. Let's say, for instance, that the performance chart shows you had a patient who left without being seen (LWBS) last night.

- Why? Answer: We couldn't get the patient into the back quick enough.
- Why? Answer: We were too full of other patients.
- Why? Answer: We weren't discharging patients quickly enough because there were so many.
- Why? Answer: We weren't staffed up for our volume of patients.
- Why? Answer: We schedule the same number of staff at every shift and do not account for day of week or time of day volume.

Keep this questioning going until you hit an actionable spot in the sequence. In this case, we can take action on the staffing level by scheduling personnel in response to observed trends in the volume of incoming patients.

As you know from experience, delays in bringing patients into the back can result from many things. Start by solving those problems that you can while in the huddle, and then assign a group to do the more complex work. Capture that work's progress on the Action Plan. See Section C of this chapter for further explanation.

Plans — What Will We Do?

The second component of the Daily Management Board is the Plans. Now that we have a feel for the problems and challenges of the organization as indicated on the Dashboard side, the Plans section is intended to engage frontline staff in resolving or improving the issues the department faces. Two primary techniques comprise this section: Improvement Action Plans and Standard Work.

The Improvement Action Plan indicates who needs to do what in order to improve performance on measures and objectives. This transforms the conversation into action. Engaging staff's active participation is essential for improving unit efficiency and effectiveness.

The Improvement Action Plan, shown in Illustration 3.4 as a part of the Daily Management Board, consists of three columns: the plan defines *what* will be done, *when* it will be done, and *who* among staff will do it. The more specifically this can be defined, the better. The *who* is always someone present at the huddle, even if the only task is to make sure someone else who is not at the huddle gets the job done. We need accountability within the group to ensure follow-through occurs; otherwise no one will do it. For example, Sally might not be the one who performs staff scheduling, but she will contact the right person to get the job done if that person is identified in the action plan. Also, having a specific date is important, rather than, for instance, a month, because a month timeframe could give someone the leeway of an entire 31 days to get the task done. Does "July" mean July 1 or July 31? How long do we actually have?

| Implementation/Action Plan | | |
|---|---|---|
| What | When | Who |

| | | | |
|---|---|---|---|
| 1. | Update process change alert for safety cross | 10/1/20xx | Pat Jones, Charge RN |
| 2. | Oder new safety rules | 10/10/20XX | Pat Jones, Charge RN |
| 3. | Update flow diagram for group | 10/15/19 | Same Barnes, CNA |

Illustration 3.4. Implementation Action Plan.

Sometimes the plan is to develop standard work. I use the term standard work to include protocols, evidenced based practices, standard procedures, etc. This term is applied to any task in which the work is prescribed by content, sequence, and time to complete the task. The Standard Work Review sheet is used by the manager or supervisor to track responsibilities. However, if a member is not meeting the standard work deadlines, the manager is made aware and can coach the individual. We first make the assumption that staff who are not following standard work do so because they do not understand the importance of standard work. This, in turn, may indicate several things: they were not adequately trained on the new standard; they have not habituated into using it (it takes time to develop new habits); and/or the standard work itself is inadequate and needs to be adjusted in order to be more effective.

Rather than jumping to conclusions, dig deeper into the *why* in order to better understand the reason the staff member is not using the standard work. There should be positive recognition at the huddle and during individual performance reviews of those staff members who have used the new standard of work. It's important to acknowledge when desired behaviors are being met and reinforced.

The Process Change Alert is exactly that—it alerts staff to changes made to the standard work, including modifications to procedures and protocols. Likely, a process change is the result of an action item to revisit their standard work and make adjustments to it. Section D on standard work will go into much more detail about this subject.

Illustration 3.5. Huddles.

Section B: Huddles

The term huddle derives from its use in football games where the team gets together quickly to come up with the next play, or plan of action, based upon progress down the field of play. Notice how football teams use many visual cues or control tools to monitor and manage that progress. Instead of a scoreboard, in Lean we use the Daily Management Board to monitor, manage, and improve performance on key department measures. We make a distinction between a Daily Management Board and a huddle (versus calling it a huddle *board*), for the same reason we make a distinction between a football scoreboard and huddle. The huddle is the activity to focus our efforts based on measured performance.

The intent here is for the unit's staff to meet, review the data, and discuss what and how to improve—quickly. As such, unit huddles should be focused and brief. They should review what has occurred during the last 24 hours and define what unit staff will do in the next 24 hours *and after*. That does not exclude longer-term actions, but the emphasis for huddles is brevity: they should not last longer than 15 minutes. Operational unit huddles do not replace staff meetings, nor do they replace clinical huddles, which are focused on specific clinical and patient care concerns. These operational huddles are focused on daily operations. They are also a great opportunity to *identify* improvements to processes and operations that can be worked in greater detail later, such as in a Lean workshop.

Especially in the early implementation of DMBs and huddles, it is important to identify issues within the control of the workgroup that can be resolved quickly. We want both to experience a sense of accomplishment and empowerment, and also to learn the skills of group problem solving.

At first, managers and staff sometimes confuse addressing a particular issue for a particular patient with addressing process-related or systemic issues. In other words, they confuse clinical with operational issues. It is important to keep them separate and distinct from one another. The clinical aspect of an issue—for example, someone falling and hurting themselves the previous night—is discussed during clinical huddles to determine if more actions are required for that particular patient. However, the operational side of this event, discussed during the huddle, addresses the question of how to prevent these *types* of falls from occurring again. So, we use the particular situation to talk about the general process by which we get work done. Huddles are, therefore, the active engagement of staff in the overall improvement of safety, quality, and processes.

Of course, not everything can be discussed and resolved in 15 minutes. If an issue requires more research or thought than can be done in 15 minutes, it is completely legitimate to assign that issue to a smaller group who, in turn, will come back to a subsequent huddle with the information required for group decision-making. Another option is to assemble a team to use a Kaizen event to look more deeply at a more complex or chronic issue. The huddles, in effect, also become a coordinating activity to oversee improvements done outside huddle time.

If you conduct internal staff satisfaction surveys, and the hospital or departments consistently rate low in "Engaged Workforce," then it is possible you are not taking advantage of huddles or their equivalent in order to engage staff. While analogous to the daily safety huddle that many hospitals use, this particular approach of using the Daily Management Board is specific to each unit, and

78

augments and incorporates (as defined above) more priorities and measures.

How frequent should huddles be? Doing huddles *daily* is usually too big of a leap for most units to incorporate into their workday. I recommend starting out once a week. In a year, that can mean 52 times as many occasions for departments and units to actively improve their operations. Then, as the huddles begin to result in improved workflow, clinical outcomes, increased patient satisfaction, and increased staff satisfaction, you can increase the frequency of huddle use. Done right, the effectiveness of huddles will result in wanting to do them more frequently. But seriously, huddles should last no more than 15 minutes at most.

Where to keep the Daily Management Board (DMB) and to conduct the huddles is best decided by the group. Keep in mind, you want it easily accessible by the group, easy to see, and comfortable for having conversation without disturbing or being interrupted by others. I have known units to use break rooms, conference rooms, managers' offices, and even hallways. Adjust the structure of the DMB to meet the physical requirements of your area.

## Sequence of Huddle Discussions

The following is a numbered description of what I have experienced as the best sequence for discussing the elements of a

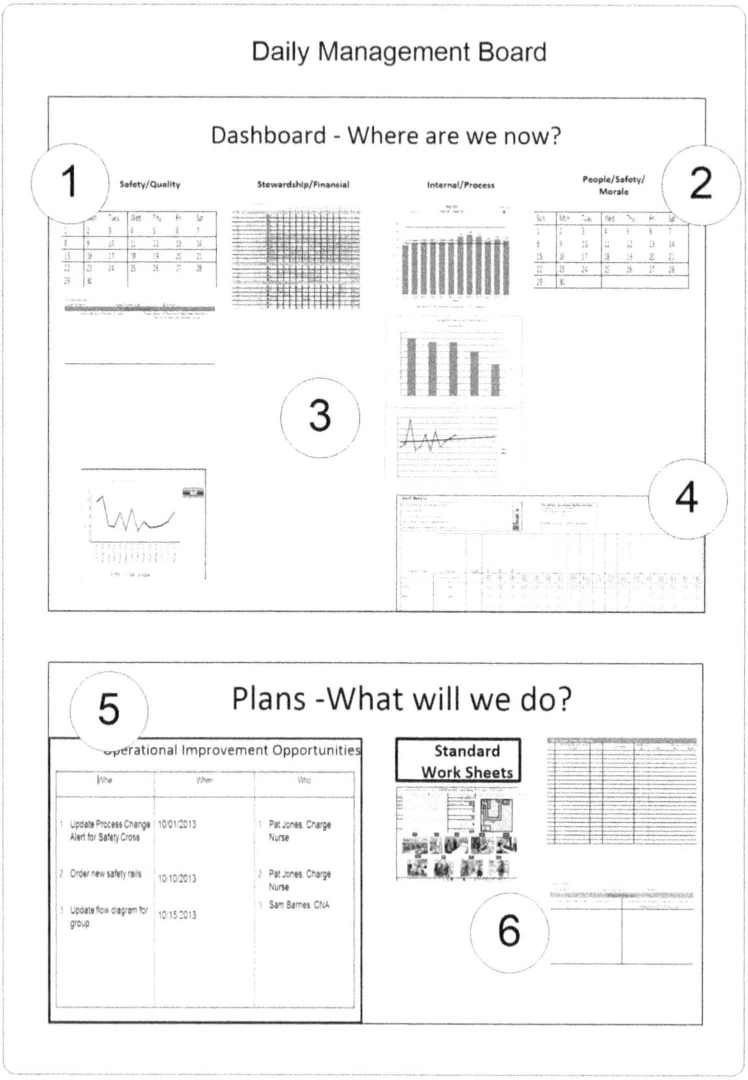

Illustration 3.6. Sequence of Huddle at Daily Management Board.

Daily Management Board while conducting a huddle (Illustration 3.6). Keep in mind that the exact format and layout of a DMB must be decided by the unit, but all of the elements should exist, and the discussion should progress as described below. Because there was a huge emphasis on safety in our hospital system, we considered safety to be a "Quality" measure and a "People" measure, hence its appearance twice. We believed that quality care started with safe care, and safe care began with safe employee practices. The old expression, "Start and end with safety" really applied. So, that's where we began all conversations in the huddle, too.

1. Safety for Patients

Most hospitals are focused on safety first; therefore, that is generally the most logical first measure. From the left side of the Dashboard, start with patient safety measures (in the Quality column) and the existence and severity of safety events affecting patients in your department. Included on the Safety Calendar page should be the definition of a safety event, the criteria for each level,

and a list of instances in which a negative safety event occurred (Illustration 3.7). This is also a good time to talk about any patient safety alerts that might exist.[15]

Discussing safety first is intended to reinforce that a safe patient experience and a safe work environment are the essential ingredients to successful patient care. Start at the upper left (1) to discuss any patient safety events. Start with the particulars of what happened with that patient. Then ask the question, "How do we prevent this type of incident from occurring again?" As mentioned before, if the ways to prevent this type of incident from recurring are not obvious to the group during the huddle, then assign the task to someone in the group to go research and bring back results of the investigation to a later huddle.

| 1 | 2 | 3 | 4 | 5 | 6 | 7 |
|---|---|---|---|---|---|---|

---

[15] The discussion here about safety is separate from the practice of most hospitals to have a hospital-wide safety meeting attended by managers. This example is unit-specific, and is an addition to the hospital's general safety meeting. There is, furthermore, a health care industry-wide accepted format that we used that I do not present here to respect copyright and proprietary rights.

| 8 | 9 | 10 | 11 | 12 | 13 | 14 |
|---|---|----|----|----|----|----|
| 15 | 16 | 17 | 18 | 19 | 20 | 21 |
| 22 | 23 | 24 | 25 | 26 | 27 | 28 |
| 29 | 30 | | | | | |
| Green = Safe Day | | | | | | |
| Yellow = Near Hit | | | | | | |
| Orange = Precursor to a Safety Event | | | | | | |
| Red = Serious Safety Event | | | | | | |
| Event Criteria: | | | | | | |

2. Safety for Staff

Then, move to the upper right (2) to discuss any staff safety events under the People column. The patient and staff safety measures are different, but equally important, and specific potential safety concerns must be identified by each unit. For example, Critical Care might be monitoring safety concerns such as back strains, sharps events, and aggressive patients. Mental Health and ED might measure violent attacks by patients toward staff.

3. Stewardship and Internal

Next, we move to the department's financial data. Displaying the department's financials is useful to remind everyone that costs and revenue are directly tied to the financial health of the department. Not to mention their getting paid, being able to hire more staff, or purchase needed equipment. Even in non-profit organizations, the hospital must exceed expenses with revenue, or the hospital will cease to operate. A productivity measure could also be displayed, since it is tied to operating costs.

Internal measures are directly connected to how efficiently the department is operating. Lean and process improvement methods work because of the belief that our results and outcomes are only as good as the processes that make them. We use the "internal" label because we are looking at how we do our work. At this level, we are measuring processes such as admitting and discharging patients in a timely and effective manner. We are also keeping track of how

82

accurately we do our scheduling, how often we start on time, how quickly and thoroughly we are cleaning the rooms, how accurately we place the right patient in the right bed from ED to IP, etc.

It is not uncommon to show the next higher level of measures, such as average length of stay (ALOS) and left without being seen (LWBS) or late starts, on the Daily Management Board in conjunction with the staff-level measures. This can help staff to see leadership's priorities, such as the overall strategic goals of the hospital or department, as well as the specific goals, issues, or concerns that the unit is facing. Most managers must go through a few iterations of adjusting management measures before everyone agrees upon the relevance and appropriateness of the frontline measure.

4. People

The fourth topic in the huddle sequence is training and certification, which goes under the People column. Ensuring that appropriate training and certification is kept current is absolutely essential to maintaining a highly skilled workforce. Pay attention to opportunities for staff to obtain additional certifications that will heighten your staff's self-esteem, their ability to contribute to the unit and hospital, and their ability to provide the best possible patient care (another form of Respect for People). Illustration 3.8 provides an example of a simple matrix format to track all training and certification requirements.

|  | Name | Name | Name | Name |
|---|---|---|---|---|
| **Class** | Mary | Clarisse | Yvonne | John |
| Special instruments handling | X |  |  |  |
| Sterilization techniques | X |  | X |  |

| | | | | |
|---|---|---|---|---|
| Radiation protection guidance | X | | X | X |
| Mass casualty incident handling | | | X | X |
| Cardiac defibrillation | | X | X | X |
| Cardiac massage | | X | X | |
| Oxygen administration | | X | X | |

Illustration 3.8. Training and Certification Matrix.

5.  Implementation Action Plans

After discussing all of the issues, problems, and concerns that need improvement, in this section we turn those issues into action. If there is a safety event, this is where the plans to prevent it from occurring again are captured. Similarly, it is also where we identify length of stay (LOS) issues as well as possible issues of training and certification.

As mentioned before, the Implementation/Action Plan, shown again in Illustration 3.9, is a critical aspect of success, so be as specific as possible on *what* needs to be done, *by whom* in the group, and on what specific *date*. If the action is to "set up training," does that mean developing the materials and putting them into PowerPoints, or does it mean contacting someone else to do the training? Ambiguity comes from the lack of specificity, so it is important to be as specific as possible.

| Action Plan | | |
|---|---|---|
| What | Who | When |
| 1.  Set up training | Salisha Smith, RN with Franklin Pierce (Educator) | 10/1/20xx |

84

| | | |
|---|---|---|
| • Determine content of training, coordinate with Education<br>• Develop PPT<br>• Trial run class<br>• Schedule staff<br>• Conduct class | | |

Illustration 3.9. Implementation Action Plan.


6. Standard Work

The most common output of any improvement activity should be the creation of a standard work that is implemented, refined, and used to train and review everyone's work. We use the following criteria to guide us in the creation of standard work: it must identify the *content* of the work, that is, the individual steps to be taken. It must identify the *sequence* in which the work is to be done. And, as much as possible, standard work should identify the *amount of time* each step in that sequence requires. See Section D of this chapter for more details on standard work.

A checklist is a simple example of standard work, especially if the time required for each step is taken into consideration. Protocols are standard work. Evidence-based practices are standard work. The forms and formats for standard work are infinite. The main point is to establish, among everyone doing the work, a consensus as to *how* the work will be done each time and by each person doing the process.

This section of the DMB is used to maintain a copy of all standard work created. It should define the criteria by which managers review the implementation of the standard work, and it should announce any changes that have been made to it as well. If changes are not being made to standard work, it is usually because people aren't fully implementing them and simultaneously asking, "How can we do this even better?"

Everyone should be aware of any procedural changes before they are implemented. The huddle, therefore, is a great opportunity to inform staff of such changes.

## Section C: Improvement Teams

## Types of Decision-Making Teams

I use the terms *teams* and *meetings* interchangeably because, to me, they form a continuum of decision-making, or, they should, at least. I've often been asked what the difference between a facilitated workshop and a facilitated meeting is. I usually don't distinguish between them; the reason is that any time we get a group of people together to discuss an issue or resolve a problem, we should be making a decision. I view most information-sharing meetings as a waste of time.

In turn, the decision to be made dictates the agenda — or *how* the decision will be made. And how the decision will be made dictates the length of the meeting. If it is a relatively straightforward decision, such as who will lead the new project or who will implement the new process today, then a shorter meeting is more appropriate; in contrast, decisions about how to improve the existing onboarding process, or how to redesign the flow of patients in the emergency department, could take several days.

When designing agendas, be aware of who needs to be present, because that will also help guide the relative time needed to reach the decision(s). More people in a meeting means the meeting requires more time.

The point is that the purpose and function of getting people together should be more organic: you assemble a team together based upon what you are trying to accomplish, not based upon what the meeting type is called. I use types here as a mere convenience, not as a rigid formula.

You may recall my statement earlier that a facilitator's job is to manage the conversation in order to manage decision-making. Think about the types of meetings as a continuum of importance, impact, and complexity in regards to the decision being made, who makes it, and how it is to be made. Whether a meeting is necessary, and how long it should be are central pieces of advice your facilitator should provide.

There are six general types of teams or meetings that can be used to accomplish your objectives. The last one was added as a direct result of my experience at the hospital system. In other words, it was a new way to consider how to conduct these meetings.

1. Just Do Its
2. Ongoing meetings
3. Facilitated meetings
4. Problem solving meetings
5. Kaizen events
6. Extended events

The main distinguishing characteristic across these six types is *how long the group needs to meet*. Again, what you want to accomplish should dictate the type and length of workshop. Regardless of the type of team, I highly recommend being as inclusive as possible. I would rather apologize for wasting someone's time than apologize for not including someone I should have. Illustration 3.10 summarizes the six decision-making team types, their purpose, and their typical duration.

| Type of Decision Making Teams/Meetings | Purpose | Typical Duration |
|---|---|---|
| 1. Just Do It | To take action on an obviouse course of action. | Immediate and ASAP |
| 2. Ongoing Meetings | To meet regularly to make decisions about the business, operations, Patient care ect. This type of meeting handles the ongoing work of the organization. | 15 minutes - 1 hour |
| 3. Faciliated Meetings | To reach a dicision on a tightly bound issue that requires a short period of time, but time is of the essence of getting the dicision made by those afftected or are major stackholders- usually cross functional or cross-department. | 1-4 hours |
| 4. Problem Solving Meetings | To reach a decision that will require a more developed implementation plan and standard work identified. Usually solution set does not lend itself to a pilot or trial run. | 8-16 hours (two days) |
| 5. Kaizen Teams / Events | The issue is complex enough that people from different departments or functions are needed and there is time or need to trial run the solutions/countermeasures. | 24-40+ hours |
| 6. Extended Events | The issue is truly complex and will likely require several stakeholders to buy-in to the countermeasures. No one "event" will successfully ensure successful implementation | 12+ weeks of one-day meetings |

Illustration 3.10. Types of Decision-Making Teams.

1. **Just-Do-Its (JDIs)**. Sometimes, we already know the answer to a problem, but have just not gathered, recognized, and implemented it. We don't need deep analysis when the answer to an issue is obvious. Everyone agrees to it. Let's just do it! For example, we know we need to fix the printer. Someone calls it in. Or, we are out of a supply item. Someone calls it in! The point is that sometimes we don't need a complex committee to solve a problem. This mode of decision-making is frequently seen at the huddle because of the short nature of the problem being solved and the resources needed to solve it.

2. **Ongoing meetings** are your typical staff meetings, board meetings, clinical hand-offs, or any meeting where a regular rhythm needs to be established to discuss issues and make decisions. See Appendix A for an example of a generic agenda for an ongoing meeting.

89

3. **Facilitated meetings** are typically 1-4 hour meetings, focused on a tightly bound issue. This group does not necessarily need all of the various Lean or meeting tools required of a typical improvement team, but could use the help of a skilled facilitator to stay focused. See Appendix B for an example agenda for a facilitated meeting.

4. **Problem solving teams** are typically 8-16 hours long, and their product might be a set of solutions (called "countermeasures" in Lean lingo) including standard work and an implementation plan. More than likely, this type of team has little time to conduct a trial run, or the outcome of the meeting is such that no trial run can be done. For instance, if the intent is to develop a new surgery program, the stakes may be too high to experimentally "test out" the plan prior to actually implementing it, because patients' lives are at stake. See Appendix C for an example agenda for a one-day problem solving team. An example topic that would benefit from this type of meeting would be creating a standard Emergency Department (ED) to Inpatient (IP) bed slip for admitting patients.

The two main criteria for deciding if an issue needs to be elevated to an improvement team (versus handled while *in* a huddle) are:

- If the issue is big enough that it can't be handled in the 15-minute window of a huddle, or even as a separate action item.
- If the issue identified affects more than one function or department.

Working across functions or departments usually requires scheduling time with the other function(s) to work on resolving the issue(s). This doesn't mean the teams have to meet for hours upon hours. A simple 1-2 hour meeting might suffice, but it usually exceeds the context of an operational huddle.

If the team is focused on improving processes, procedures, protocols, and practices, then the outcome of the team should be a solution set, or countermeasure. It should include standard work or changes to existing standard work, as well as an implementation plan that includes the "check and adjust" meetings required to ensure implementation is sustained.

The two major outcomes of Kaizen teams and extended events should always be standard work and an implementation plan.

5. **Kaizen events**. Though they go by different names in different regions of the country (Rapid Process Improvement Workshop, Rapid Improvement Events, Lean Events, Accelerated Improvement Team, etc.), the main distinction that I make between problem solving teams and Kaizen events is that a Kaizen event is longer (3-5 days) and oftentimes allows a trial period for a countermeasure. See Appendix D for an example agenda of a Rapid Process Improvement Workshop (or Kaizen event).

The most common reason a Kaizen team gets created is that a high-level leader (director, vice-president, president, COO, etc.) recognizes that an issue is so big or chronic that it requires the concentrated effort of several people across more than one clinical unit. The leader will ask to bring together a group of cross-functional subject matter experts (SMEs) in order to tackle a larger, more complex problem or process issue.

A variation on this format is to hold 3-5 one-day sessions across as many weeks. For example, I might do two one-day sessions separated by a week or two, or have four one-day sessions separated by a week each. That way, I can adjust the time allotted for the sessions, or even revisit the need to meet all four times, giving the managers time to adjust the work schedule.

An example of a topic that would benefit from this type of meeting would be improving the process of getting patients from triage through registration and into a bed.

The advantage of this approach is that the team can check in with and inform their workgroup about what they are doing and get in-progress feedback on suggested changes. The disadvantage is that the team will need to revisit issues to get back up to speed on the task at hand, or worse, the team may lose momentum in between meetings. Sometimes team continuity is a challenge, as members that attended one session may not be able to attend the other.

In one case, the ED and IP teams were so effective at working together that we completed the Kaizen event in less time than we had anticipated. Since one of the major issues that delayed admitting patients was locating supplies, we finished the final draft of the Admit Process Standard Work, and shifted to doing 5S in the Emergency Department supply rooms during that last two days.

6. **Extended events** are another method based on the same premise as Kaizen events, except that the teams meet for an entire day, once a week, for 10-13 weeks. Like Kaizen events, extended events allow time to trial run the solution set, including the new standard work.

A significant advantage to this approach is that in between workshop sessions team members can go to the unit and test their standard work or other improvement ideas. Because the format of conducting an extended event is unique to most organizations, and because there are a lot more moving parts to conducting extended events, the entirety of Chapter 4 is devoted to a detailed explanation and roadmap for conducting them.

Critical Success Factors for Team Effectiveness

Experience has reinforced for me that the best guarantors of team success are the following:

1. **Strong and visible sponsorship.** The sponsor is the person with the authority to approve and implement the changes recommended by the team. Without strong, authoritative sponsorship, starting a project would be a waste of everyone's time.

2. **Having the right people in the room**, no matter how many that has to be. There are three criteria for who the "right" people are. First are subject matter experts (SMEs). These are people that thoroughly know the topic to be discussed. This also means that they are typically frontline employees who work with the process every day and have done so for years. The goal is to have the final solution(s) be adopted; thus, it is essential to include credible frontline SMEs to create and sustain the countermeasures.

New employees can also be invaluable here because they frequently can see where the problems are in the process that the experienced employees can no longer see. New employees fall into the category of what I somewhat whimsically call SMNs (pronounced "smins"). These are Subject Matter Novices, and they are the new folks who can sometimes see with more clarity all of the workarounds and problems that others have long since taken for granted as the way things get done. Oftentimes, they are newcomers to the organization and do not have a vested interest in maintaining the status quo, so they can provide wonderful insight into the workarounds, issues, and brokenness to which others have long become accustomed. They are your antidote to the SMEs who sometimes fall into the "that's the way we've always done it" mindset. Of course, it is important to include both SMEs and SMNs in the improvement process.

3. **Having an influencer on the team** will help in the long run. This means frontline staff who are a part of the day-to-day delivery of the process and can influence their peers. Key influencer(s) need to be on the team to help sell the "solution" to others. Preferably, these people are also positive and motivated to make a change. Though we are not necessarily looking for early adopters, as early adopters are already inclined to accept change. Consider including people who may need more convincing but who will be a strong advocate for the countermeasure once convinced. Ideally, they convince themselves as part of the teamwork process. Ideally, too, the rationale for the improvement processes should be self-evident.

This can be a tough balancing act because we don't want to exclude from the team someone who could help immeasurably but who simply hasn't yet bought in to the new changes. Conversely, we don't want to include people on the team if they will be disruptive or ineffective. This is a situational and person-specific judgment call.

4. **Permission to act.** Though all recommendations need sponsorship approval, this approval should be a formality. If you have picked the right people and have carefully defined the scope of the project with a charter, then approval is a given. If not, then

leadership needs to reassess their projects, parameters, and team-member selecting abilities.

In Chapter 4, I discuss the role and function of using a charter to help articulate these four critical factors of sponsorship, team member selection, influencers, and process approval.

For those who complain that there are too many people on the team, it simply means they don't understand the nature of change management. It is not how good the solution is that matters as much as the willingness of frontline staff to implement the solution. I would take great support for a mediocre answer over no support for the best answer.

Keep in mind a famous Lean expression: "Better now, perfect later." In this context, it means that if I can get staff to start making improvements to the process, and I have ongoing "check and adjust" meetings, then no matter the quality of the initial countermeasure, we will continue to improve upon it. It is the engagement of frontline that is as much our goal in the beginning as the actual improvement itself.

Section D: Standard Work

Why is it important to have consistent standard work in healthcare? (Illustration 3.11 is an example of Standard Work) Preventable medical errors persist as the number three killer in the United States — third only to heart disease and cancer — claiming the lives of some 400,000 people each year.[16]

Based on my experience working in hospitals for over eight years, I believe that one of the major reasons for these medical errors is the lack of using standard work. Even though standard work exists in the form of protocols, evidenced-based practices, checklists, charts, and forms, there is not a strict adherence to these standards.

In 2001, American Airlines Flight 587 crashed into the Queens neighborhood of Belle Harbor, New York, killing 265. From 2001 to

---

[16] James, John T. "A New, Evidence-based Estimate of Patient Harms Associated with Hospital Care." *Journal of Patient Safety*. Volume 9, Issue 3. September 2013: 122-128.

2018, however, United States airline companies had not seen a large plane crash with major loss of life. In spite of these occasional tragedies, there is a reason that flying is statistically the safest mode of transportation: the implementation of and strict adherence to standard procedures.

One day I spoke with a pilot seated beside me on a flight home. I had always thought that the two pilots in the cockpit usually worked together, kind of like the stereotypical TV "police partners" in a squad car. He informed me otherwise: he said he rarely works with the same co-pilot twice. He won't know who will be beside him until he shows up for the flight. "Then how can you work together as a team? How will you know what they are going to do?" I asked. "Because I know what to expect from my co-pilot. They will have been taught to do the exact same thing the exact same way, each and every time," he replied. "And what if he decides not to follow the routine?" I asked. "We have reporting mechanisms to make sure we all follow the same safe flying procedures." I was unaware of this.

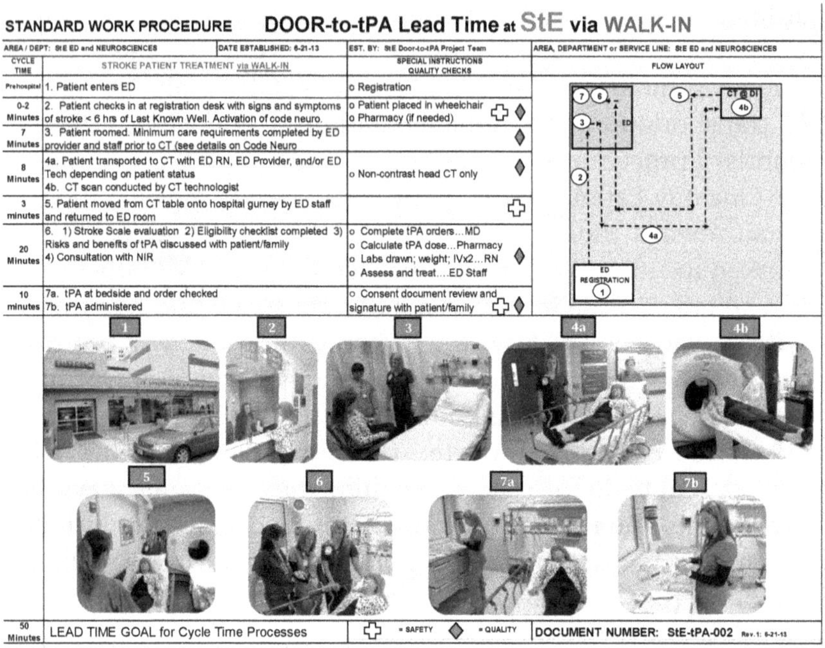

Illustration 3.11. Standard Work.

It got me thinking about the reaction I've had many times from doctors when I have discussed or taught standard work. "You mean cookie-cutter medicine?" They sometimes ask. So, I have finally found a good response that requires asking a few questions back. It goes something like this:

"First, let me say that, yes, I do believe in cookie-cutter medicine. And so do you. When you say cookie-cutter medicine, do you mean that everyone does the same procedure for diagnosing and treating the same way?"

"Yes."

"Then, by this definition, wouldn't evidence-based practices and protocols be considered cookie-cutter medicine? Would you not agree that we want to perform infection control, administer oxygen to patients with COPD, measure blood pressure noninvasively in children, etc. in the same way?

Medical protocols are intended to allow for a systematic approach to a condition. They exist to make sure serious mistakes and variations are not made in treatment, and to ensure that correct investigations are asked for. A contemporary, well-documented method of treatment is instituted, and cost effectiveness is thusly maintained. Litigation, furthermore, may be prevented as well through consistency of practice. A surgical safety checklist developed by Haynes et al. for the World Health Organization is an example of a protocol that can be useful before, during, and after surgery to reduce morbidity and mortality in a global population.[17] Protocols or checklists can and should be used when there is some leeway for a procedural approach.

The director of one of our OBGYN departments said this about the use of a standard protocol for deliveries: "Research has shown that vaginal births result in fewer complications than surgical delivery by Cesarean section. Therefore, we will all follow the same protocol for vaginal birth delivery. This does not preclude you from using your best medical judgment should a Cesarean be necessary, but I want you to fully justify it in the patient's chart. You do not need to justify vaginal birth."

I taught new hire orientation to thousands of people for over eight years at a hospital system. Every single time, I asked, "how many of you are being taught to do the exact same job by more than one person?" Usually about 75% would raise their hands. I would then ask, "How many of you are being taught to do that same job the same way by two or more people?" In seven years not one hand stayed up. *Not one.* And they all admitted that they took the best practices from their "teachers" and created their own.

---

[17] Haynes, Alex, et al. "A Surgical Safety Checklist to Reduce Morbidity and Mortality in a Global Population." *The New England Journal of Medicine.* Volume 360. January 29, 2009: 491-499.

The way doctors and nurses practice is the way they were taught, and they were all taught at different schools, so they only know what they know. That's true for all of us: we only know what we know.

But can you expect predictable results from people doing the same job different ways? No. The problem is if we can't predict what someone else did, then we either have to take on faith that they did their part right, or we have to start over to make sure everything was done right. Imagine this self-correcting happening thousands of times a day in your organization. Can you see the increasing likelihood of wasting time and money? Can you anticipate defects in the process that can cause physical harm to patients? The impetus of the 5 Million Lives Campaign, for example, was actually to institute more evidence-base practices and medical protocols.[18] That is, use more cookie cutters!

A major insight that I've gained from one of my past employees at this hospital system was to finish any workshop or event with the creation or modification of standard work. Because of the success he was having with his teams using standard work, it became apparent that this was a necessary product of any team's efforts.

While limitless in how it is formatted, standard work provides an excellent mechanism for gaining agreement on how the work will be done, sustained, taught, and managed. The key factors of good standard work is that it contain the *content, sequence*, and *duration* of each step. In one document, you have the means to talk about changes to the process and get feedback. You can teach new people how to do the same job the same way, and advise managers to adhere to the standard work while coaching employees to meet those standards.

Without standard work, teams don't often agree on actual steps, particularly where there are differences of opinion. Writing it down in visible, clearly-articulated terms matters on several levels: safety,

---

[18] Berwick, Donald, "Initiatives," *Institute for Healthcare Improvement*, December 2004, http://www.ihi.org/Engage/Initiatives/Completed/5MillionLivesCampaign/Pages/default.aspx.

predictability, teach-ability, replication, and enhancement of performance. Illustration 3.12 is an example of a simple standard work protocol for radio operations:

1. At the start of shift, Tech obtain walkie talkie from charging station. The charging station is located next to room #3. Ensure it is on channel #3.
2. Tech write walkie talkie number and initial the Shift Schedule sheet (resides with Charge Nurse) and time charger taken.
3. At end of shift, return walkie talkie to the Charging Station and sign out with your initials on Shift Schedule.
4. All other walkie talkies must remain in their respective locations.

Illustration 3.12. Walkie-Talkie Standard Work Example.

Standard work should reflect the result of a team's activities that establish a best practice for how that work gets done. Most importantly, it must be constantly reviewed with staff and adjusted as staff discover and agree upon better and faster ways to obtain consistent and reliable results. Reviews can be accomplished by watching staff perform the new standard during manager rounding, or using huddles to inquire if any of the standard work procedures need to be revisited for improvement. Then, everyone must be informed, trained, and required to do it the same, new way, without exception. That is, until an improvement to the process is made again, and then re-codified in the standard work procedure. Until the next improvement. Ad infinitum.

Summary

Engaging frontline staff is best accomplished by providing them with the opportunity (the *requirement*, rather) to improve processes and customer service. The Daily Management Board, Huddles, Improvement Teams and standard work are all tried and true mechanisms for simultaneously improving how products are made and how services are delivered to improve customer quality and satisfaction. These methods and tools need to be adapted to your particular environment, but they are the essential tools of Lean, in the same way that a hammer, screwdrivers, and wrenches should be essential to anybody's toolbox. You may not use them all the time, but they are all useful and serve important functions.

It can't be reiterated enough: the one requirement of virtually every task, effort, event, workshop, etc., is for the staff to create standard work. Regardless of format, this tool is critical to stabilizing consistent processes. The importance of this is never understated by seasoned professionals in Lean.

Teams and huddles are excellent venues for engaging frontline staff as well as members of other units or departments in order to solve problems. In turn, this provides an opportunity for them to learn how to negotiate and compromise while working as team members. Ultimately, we use teams and huddles to help create a collaborative environment that goes beyond just individual teams and projects.

# Chapter 4 — Extended Events

The first section in this chapter is the high-level "Executive Overview," so that the C-suite will understand this approach, in the hopes of seeing its value and implementing it thereafter. The next section is directed at the Lean Practitioner who will lead the hospital staff through these extended events and activities. I have provided a general but detailed outline of extended events, and in order to best describe them, I have included in italics the actions that we took during our own actual events.

## Executive Overview

The extended event is an expansion of what we commonly known as Kaizen events or Rapid Process Improvement Workshops. It is a journey that starts with 2-3 months of assessment and planning, as well as several weeks of improvement team work. It is then followed by active "sustain" work, checking and adjusting as we go. The expectation is that the work will result in the creation of daily management boards and huddles, and then expand to address other issues, and possibly more intensive Kaizen, problem solving, or extended events. The intent is both to leverage the highest impact areas of major care settings, such as the emergency department, inpatient services, and perioperative services, and also to create a structure and culture for continuous improvement. The longer, more detailed version of extended events is described here.  See Illustration 4.1 for extended event steps and timelines that reflect the three phases of event planning, team work, and sustain.

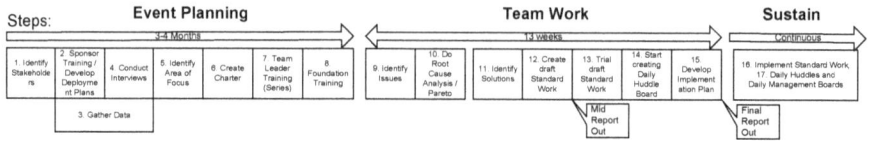

| Steps: | Event Planning | | | | | | | Team Work | | | | | | | Sustain | |
|---|---|---|---|---|---|---|---|---|---|---|---|---|---|---|---|---|
| | 3-4 Months | | | | | | | 13 weeks | | | | | | | Continuous | |
| 1. Identify Stakeholders | 2. Sponsor Training / Develop Deployment Plans | 4. Conduct Interviews | 5. Identify Area of Focus | 6. Create Charter | 7. Team Leader Training (Series) | 8. Foundation Training | | 9. Identify Issues | 10. Do Root Cause Analysis / Pareto | 11. Identify Solutions | 12. Create draft Standard Work | 13. Trial draft Standard Work | 14. Start creating Daily Huddle Board | 15. Develop Implementation Plan | 16. Implement Standard Work, 17. Daily Huddles and Daily Management Boards | |
| | 3. Gather Data | | | | | | | | | | | | Mid Report Out | | Final Report Out | |

Illustration 4.1. Extended Events Steps.

A distinct advantage of this approach is that the hospitals benefit from not having to pull staff off the floor for 3-5 days at a time. Simply put, extended events require about one and a half days a week, for a total of 13 sessions.

The role for leadership in an extended event, and any type of process improvement project for that matter, is often different than other aspects of their job.  Sponsors must be trained in their roles and responsibilities in this new capacity.  To not train the sponsors and leadership of the hospital is to do them a great disservice.  The sooner this sponsor training and plan development session can occur after the charters have been developed, the better.  Sponsorship training and plan development is exactly that: both training and planning.  Ideally, this training will occur *before* the charter is developed.

The first part of the journey is to decide in which areas to do process improvement.  Despite differences between hospitals, most would benefit from focusing improvement activities on one or all of three areas: the emergency department, inpatient areas (and the transition from one to the other), and the operating room/perioperative services.  As a leader, you will play a significant role in deciding where to invest your and your staff's improvement resources.

*At the hospital system where I was working, we decided to focus our efforts in the following areas and in the following sequence: 1) in the emergency department; 2) the inpatient areas; and 3) the operating room/perioperative services. In the emergency department, we took into consideration emergency throughput, length of stay, number of patients who leave without being seen, and collections at the point of service. In inpatient areas, we evaluated inpatient throughput, improving bed assignments, improving discharge efficiency, and decreasing length of stay and overage days for specific patient sub-populations. For inpatient areas, too, we examined appropriate and inappropriate ICU utilization in order to improve efficiency and effectiveness of case management. Finally, in the OR/perioperative services, we took into consideration scheduling, cost of supplies, throughput, timeliness of service, and 24-hr cancellations.*

Extended Events Details

The description of extended events includes a description of the forms, tools, and methods that are used throughout this journey. Illustration 4.2 represents the complete life cycle of the extended event. It also serves as a visual checklist of the steps needed throughout, and examples of tools that will support each step. As before, while not legible, the purpose is to show the whole journey. Each section will be displayed legibly and described below.

My hope is that you will understand both how to implement an extended event as well as how to establish a ready set of tools with which to begin your journey. As mentioned before, you will discover through your own experience which tools and methods work best for you; this is simply the starting blueprint for success. I have chosen 13 weeks as the duration of extended events for the consistency of the description. However, you might find that a few weeks longer or shorter works best for you.

The following is the general outline of the activities with which to prepare the team, and to create the structures and plans for the organization to be successful during and after the team's efforts. Some of the following activities can be done concurrently. For purposes of simplicity and illustration, we will use examples of an extended event applied to the ED and IP.

General Outline of Extended Events

A. Event Planning
   1. Identify stakeholders who might be affected by the changes.
   2. Conduct sponsorship training and develop deployment plans.
   3. Collect data to refine area of focus.
   4. Conduct interviews with stakeholders.
   5. Identify specific area of focus.
   6. Create charter.
   7. Conduct team leader training.
   8. Conduct foundational training.
B. Team Work
   1. Typical Week/Meetings
   2. Extended Event 13-Week Schedule and Topics
   3. Extended Events Tools
      a. Process Flow Diagram
      b. Four-Step Problem Solving
      c. Standard Work
      d. Daily Management Boards
   4. Final Report Outs
C. Post-Extended Event Activities
   1. Use plan, do, check, adjust (PDCA).
   2. Conduct huddles at Daily Management Board.
   3. Hold additional workshops as needed.
   4. Conduct governing meetings.

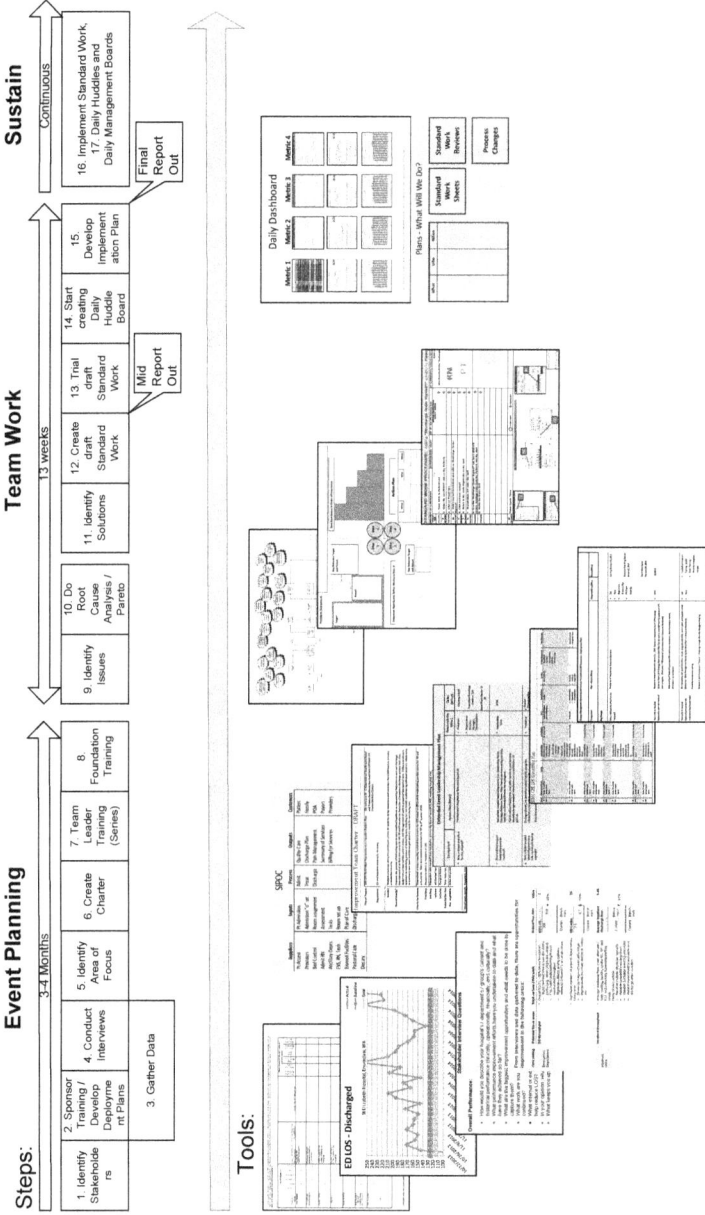

Illustration 4.2 Extended Events Steps and Tools

A. Event Planning

**1.  Identify stakeholders who might be affected by the changes.**

A comprehensive identification of the stakeholders (those who will in some way be affected by the changes that will be made) is critical to making sure that the right people are included for the right reasons (Illustration 4.3).

When most executives and managers first start improvement work, they try to figure out the *lowest* number of people who should be involved and engaged.  That is a mistake.  Remember, it is not about the quality of the solution that will determine success, but the quality of the buy-in by those who must implement, adjust, and sustain the changes.  Too often we view Lean events in isolation as a standalone project.  It is not just a project; you are using extended events and other improvement activities as part of an overall culture change.  We are on the journey of engaging employees, teaching collaborative decision-making, teaching people to be experimenters, and making it okay to learn from experience.

Stakeholder analysis is useful for identifying both who will be affected and how much they will be affected.  It will help identify who should be interviewed in the third step of collecting data: who should be informed throughout, who should be represented on the team, who should be trained, etc.  I recommend that the stakeholder analysis be done by the executives and key event planners for each of the major areas (such as ED, IP and OR) that are being improved to ensure everyone affected is kept informed of the changes.

*The deviation that we found most useful, in doing the stakeholder analysis, was to merge it with the Six Sources of Influence described in Chapter 1.  In Illustration 4.3, the left side of the stakeholder analysis follows typical formatting. Where the format deviates from typical is in the addition of the last six columns.  Here we added the Six Sources of Influence as a sort of checklist to make sure that, for all groups of stakeholders, we thoroughly address each source of influence. This helps us to think comprehensively about our actions.*

## Stake Holder Engagement Plan

| Stakeholder / Group | Level of Engagement | | | | | | Issues / Concerns for this Stakeholder | Potential "Win(s)" for this Stakeholder | Action Plan for Improvement | Which Source of Influence does this action address? | | | | | |
| | Unaware | Aware | Understand | Collaborate | Commit | Advocate | | | | Personal Motivation | Personal Ability | Peer Motivation | Peer Ability | Structural Motivation | Structural Ability |
|---|---|---|---|---|---|---|---|---|---|---|---|---|---|---|---|
| | | | | | | | | | | | | | | | |
| | | | | | | | | | | | | | | | |
| | | | | | | | | | | | | | | | |
| | | | | | | | | | | | | | | | |
| | | | | | | | | | | | | | | | |
| | | | | | | | | | | | | | | | |

Key: O = Current state  √ = Desired future state

Illustration 4.3 Stakeholder Engagement Plan with Six Sources

A word of caution about using these last six columns: frequently, those using the six sources overstate the impact the action will have on the sources.  For example, training might impact the individual and group rows and the motivation columns (What's in it for me?), but will likely not impact the structural rows and columns.  Team members, though, will frequently want to check these off, too.


**2. Conduct sponsorship training and develop deployment plans** (3 hours). Required for sponsor, process owner, and team leaders; other managers welcome.

While the first hour is spent describing the various roles and responsibilities, the second and third hours are used to develop the leadership management plan that will support the team throughout the thirteen weeks.  A typical structure for the leader management plan is illustrated below (Illustration 4.4).  I recommend using any effective change management method to provide the structure for the components that need to be addressed.  One that I have frequently used is General Electric's "Change Acceleration Process."

The plan will need to address many areas. These include the hospital communications about the team's activities, the weekly leadership meetings, the ongoing development of the three levels of measures, the political role of the leaders in support of the team(s), and so on.   In particular, leaders need to know the following to be effective:

- The details of the extended event's timeline and structure, especially the governing measures and teams needed to monitor, implement, and sustain team progress.
- An overview of the Daily Management Board and its purpose.
- An overview of the team huddle and its functions.
- The role of managers and executives in operational rounding.

| Extended Event Leadership Management Plan | | | |
|---|---|---|---|
| Component | Action Plan (What) | Responsibility (Who) | Dates (When) |
| ☐ Who will lead this effort for the Hospital? | Presidents of Hospitals as Executive Sponsors. | ☐ President <br><br> ☐ Department Director, Manager, Team Leaders | Starting 10/16 <br><br> Executive Coaching Session: 1/8 <br><br> Team Work Starts: 2/24 |
| ☐ How will the hospital leadership team be involved? | Respective hospital leadership teams (i.e., Leadership Team, Strategy Guidance Team, Pillar Team) receive weekly/monthly updates on Extended Events team progress. <br><br> Relationship of leadership and pillar teams to one another. Identify changes needed: elimination or consolidation of groups. | ☐ Leadership Team | 2/24 |
| ☐ How will the hospital leadership serve as a role model and lead by example? | During updates, ask questions about results, progress, obstacles, action plans, and support needs <br><br> Crucial conversations training. | ☐ President | ☐ Crucial Conversation Training 2/1 <br> ☐ Monthly throughout the year |

Illustration 4.4. Leadership Management Plan.

- How to develop a plan both for supporting the team *during* the extended event and for continuing the work *after* the event concludes.

After the leaders have developed their plan, the facilitators should help augment the leader's plan with their own, and directly identify what they will do during the 13 weeks of the extended event (Illustration 4.5). This forethought is critical for the facilitator to understand their roles and responsibilities.

*The first time we did an extended event, we had not developed the facilitator plans. We spent 13 weeks guessing at what we should do next as facilitators, feeling like we were always a step behind, rather than well in front of the team. We used the weekly leader/facilitator team meetings to adjust this plan as necessary.*

*We put a lot of emphasis on learning by doing, so whenever we were training, we were "doing," and vice-versa. In this case, we were teaching*

109

*executives and managers how to be sponsors by having them develop sponsorship plans. They received a short lecture, followed immediately by application of what was taught. Expect some resistance from the executives to being "trained." When we yielded to sponsors that were "too busy" to be trained, we paid the price for the remaining period of the team's activities because of poor planning and unclear sponsorship.*

## St Elsewhere LOS Consulting Plan

| Week | Facilitator/Team Leads | Training | Team Deliverables | Communication | DMS | Leadership Team | Coaching | Physician Engagement | Other Support |
|---|---|---|---|---|---|---|---|---|---|
| 13 6/2 | • Review week Plan • Set Next Week's Agenda | | • RN to RN and CNA CNA Presentation MedSurg Manag • Standard Wo • Competencie • Training plan • .WDCP on 7 & 1 • Restructure Tre and Discharge T | • CPE Scoop (wee | • Determine PCU • Plan for DMB ro | • Cancelled | • Shane McE | • Group Health • Intensivists • Other Hospitals • Specialists • Other Attending | • |
| 14 6/9 | • Review 12 • Set Next Week's Agenda | | • Finalize DMBs (PF Bed Control) • Begin Bed Placement Standard Work • Begin MSMD Handoff | • EDThe Journey (Weekly) | DMB 8A, 8D | • DMB/DMS Rollout • Group Health • Other Hospitals • Other Specialists | • Ben • Geri • Peggy | • | • Shared Governance • Management Team |
| 15 6/16 | • Review Week Pla • Set Next Week's Agenda | | • .WDCP on EDO, MS West, 4 Sout | • The Journey (W | • DMB ED • DMB Bed Contro | • Identify and add resistance issues | • Kate • Cyril | • | |
| 16 6/23 | • Review Week Plan • Set Next Week's Agenda | | • Updated SJMC Care (formerly Collaborative Care) Standard Work | • Team The Journey (Weekly) | DMB 8B, | • Identify resistance issues | • Lori • Kathy • Wendy | • | • Shared Governance • OPLT |
| 17 6/30 | • Review Week Pla • Set Next Week's Agenda | | • .WDCP on 5 & 6 | • The Journey (W | • DMB 7, 10 | • Identify and add resistance issues | • Kim | • | |
| 18 7/7 | • Review Week Plan • Set Next Week's Agenda | | • RN to RN and CNA CNA Implementation for MedSurg • Updated SJMC Care (formerly Collaborative Care) Standard Work Out | • The Journey (Weekly) | DMB EDO, ERT, MS West, 4S | • Identify and address resistance issues | • Tessa • Josie • Richard • Stephanie • Linsay | • | • Shared Governance |
| 19 7/14 | • Review Week Pla • Set Next Week's Agenda | | • Assess Remainin Issues | • The Journey (W | • DMB 5, 6, ACC | • Identify and addre resistance issues • Start to plan tra to OPLT | • | • | |
| 20 7/21 | • Review Week Plan • Set Next Week's Agenda | | • RN to RN and CNA CNA Implementation for EDO, MSW, ACC, 10 and ERT | • The Journey (Weekly) | Validate and Sustain | • Identify and address resistance issues | | • | • Shared Governance • OPLT |

Illustration 4.5. Facilitator Consulting Support Plan.

### 3. Collect data to refine area of focus (1-4 weeks).

One of the critical requirements of doing Lean is tracking the before- and after-states so that the impact of the changes can be thoroughly measured. We wanted both subjective and objective indicators of the problems that the departments were experiencing.

We knew it would take longer to collect the quantitative data, so we started with that first.

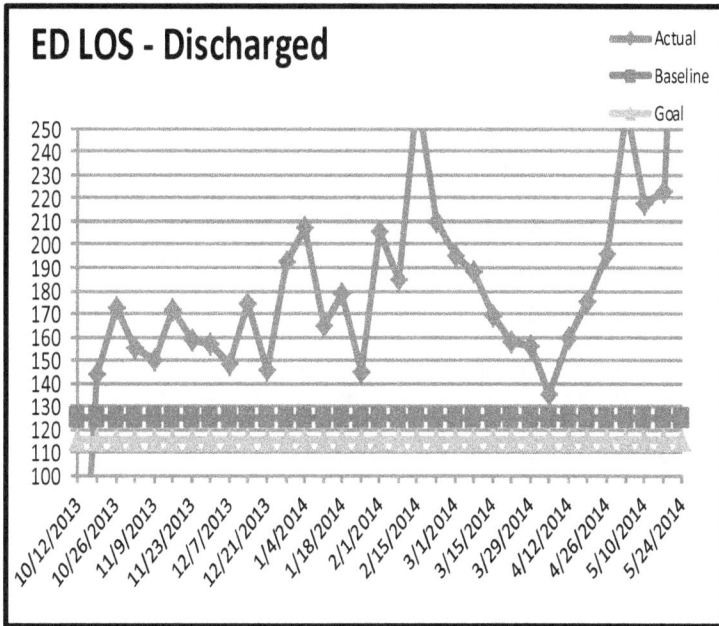

Illustration 4.6. ED LOS Trend Chart Example.

The purpose of the data collection, represented graphically in Illustration 4.6 in regards to emergency department length of stay, is to gather the *facts* about the performance of the areas you are considering for improvement. The data collection should begin as soon as the stakeholder analysis is done because this can take weeks to complete thoroughly, depending on the sophistication of your management systems and the reports that can be generated from them. Data collection and interviews (discussed in more detail in the next step) can be done concurrently.

If you have a "measures" person who can commit almost full-time to this activity, it will significantly speed up the data collection process. Expect and plan for this to take anywhere from two to 12

111

weeks if he or she is required to consult with various departments and access multiple management systems in order to get the data. Again, we found that trend charts make it easier to quickly identify areas for improvement. Up to 70% of the general population is visually oriented, so displaying information as a table can be less informative than a picture to represent the problem. Make sure the graphs are scaled the same, so the magnitude of the problems are discernable and consistent.

There are two different perspectives on whether data collection or interviews should come first. One way to look at this is to collect the data, which will tell us the areas in which to target the interviews. That is, narrow down your choices based on the data, and then enrich that objective data with subjective data from the interviews. Alternatively, interviews might help to narrow the focus of the data collection, with the premise that we want to relieve the stress staff are experiencing first, thereby getting their buy-in to other areas, perhaps more controversial or resistant ones, later.

*We have done it both ways and found collecting data before doing interviews to be more effective at keeping us focused on the areas of real — not just perceived — problems, and then enriching the data with the experience of those being interviewed. Regardless of which sequence you choose, the two together provide a more complete understanding of the direction to take.*

**4.  Conduct interviews with stakeholders** (2 days).

We have found that interviewing everyone in the same week to be most convenient. The interviews will be grouped according to the areas of focus. Remember that doctors are stakeholders and they must be interviewed, too. The interviewer should be someone who is perceived as neutral to the department(s) being interviewed. They should also be someone with whom people feel safe talking. Anonymity of the interviewee and their responses is critical here if you want accurate information, especially in an organization where staff have a tendency to place blame on each other. An excellent

112

source for the interviewers is the Operational Excellence (Lean) department staff that can help will facilitate the team work. Typical questions we asked are reflected in Illustration 4.7.

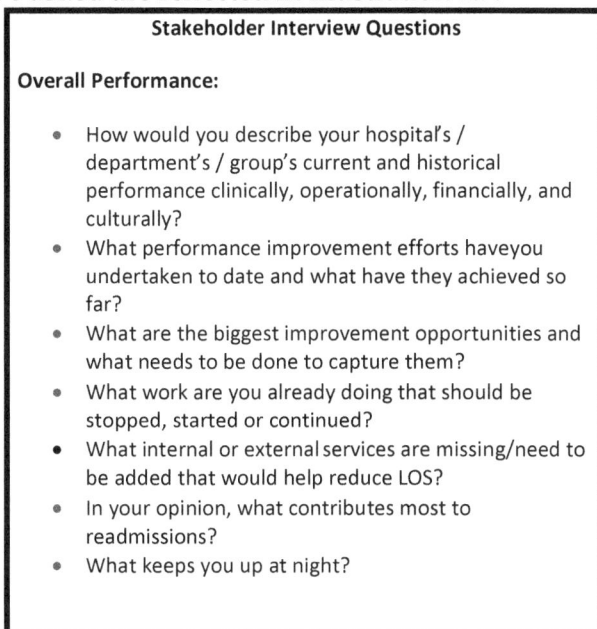

---

**Stakeholder Interview Questions**

**Overall Performance:**

- How would you describe your hospital's / department's / group's current and historical performance clinically, operationally, financially, and culturally?
- What performance improvement efforts have you undertaken to date and what have they achieved so far?
- What are the biggest improvement opportunities and what needs to be done to capture them?
- What work are you already doing that should be stopped, started or continued?
- What internal or external services are missing/need to be added that would help reduce LOS?
- In your opinion, what contributes most to readmissions?
- What keeps you up at night?

---

Illustration 4.7. Stakeholder Interview Questions.

The obvious questions at this step are: *Why not just let the data speak for itself? Why take the time to interview staff to find out where the problems are when the data clearly tells us?* There are two reasons, both equally important for obtaining subjective or experiential data. The first reason is that staff can provide a more nuanced understanding about what the data is telling us. They might point us toward other areas in which to collect performance data that might not have been obvious at first. For example, while we might want to reduce length of stay (LOS), we might also want to collect readmissions data to see if there is or will be a causal relationship between the two. The argument is often made that by reducing LOS, the quality of care will be reduced, thereby increasing readmissions. While this is

113

rarely true if the project is implemented correctly, this perception persists.

The second reason why interviews are essential is that, at the very least, they will begin to inform staff about the extended event. The more the department knows what is about to happen, the better. This should not be the only means of informing staff, but it is a good one. Plus, it will allow the Lean practitioner/team facilitator to get to know the department staff who might be on the improvement team. And, in some instances, interviews offer an opportunity to identify those who might serve well on the team. I have frequently used this as an opportunity to make suggestions about team members. Interviews begin to engage team members and demonstrate that their expertise and input is valued, which, in turn, enhances cultural change and your organization's success.

Using the performance data and interviews, select the areas that will be the focus of improvement. Keep in mind, the area you choose will undergo two journeys: first, the improvement itself, and second, the establishment of a new management system for ongoing and incremental improvements. In addition to considering the data, consider and plan for the department's willingness and ability to extensively alter the way in which work is done, as well as how front line staff will now be engaged to improve the performance of the organization through daily management boards and huddles.

**5. Identify specific area of focus** (2-3 hours).

This step helps to focus the data collection efforts and engage the stakeholders so they know what to expect. While the tools below can help narrow down the possible areas in which to focus, keep in mind that the most important factor in deciding direction is the engagement and commitment of the sponsor. Whoever has the authority to approve the changes must believe the effort is worthy. Their involvement in this selection process is key, and their time commitment and involvement in the project must be equal to the team's efforts and the time need to solve the problem - otherwise, don't invest in the effort.

Interviews and quantitative data are useful to narrow down the areas of focus (Illustration 4.8). In most cases, this information will make deciding where to apply resources quite evident. Allow time for thorough discussion. Even if the choice is obvious, there are details to discuss, as you will see below.

One of the decisions that needs to be made is how many teams will be involved. Each major area, ED and IP, will require its own team. Each team, depending upon the level of the issue's complexity and who is affected or involved, could be up to 30 people strong. For that reason, I recommend first choosing one to three areas you want to have improved, and then clearly defining the scope of those areas. Do not assume everyone knows the same starting and stopping points of a process. I have never had total agreement without discussion. That is where the SIPOC tool can be useful.

| Potential focus areas | Feedback | Supporting data |
|---|---|---|
| ED throughput | • Overall LOS is ~21% above benchmark<br>  — Significant wait time to see doc during peaks (e.g., when 20 pts are waiting)<br>  — Vertical Express Unit is underperforming in both volume and throughput<br>  — Significant delays getting patients admitted to floors/ICU at certain times | **ED LOS**, minutes<br>229<br>         180 ▼ **21%**<br><br>Current   Bench-mark |
| | • Significant numbers of patients leave without being seen<br>  — Driven by long wait times after triage<br>  — Improvement here directly affects patient satisfaction | **ED LWBS**, %<br>3.9<br>         1.0 ▼ **-75%**<br><br>Current   Bench-mark |
| Inpatient throughput | • Average discharge time is late afternoon / early evening, backing up the ED, OR, and ICU, and potentially increasing staffing needs<br>• Delay drivers include:<br>  — Need for multiple physician sign-offs<br>  — Nonstandard discharge planning processes<br>  — Nonstandard nurse practice and pace once discharge order is written | **Average inpatient discharge time,** time of day<br><br>        Before<br>3.00pm   noon ▼ **-21%**<br><br>Current   Bench-mark |

Illustration 4.8. Interview and Data Summary to Leadership.

The SIPOC tool in Illustration 4.9 sets the boundaries of the focus area. This tool helps identify the team members, including *ad hoc* members who will be necessary to improve the process.

## SIPOC

| Suppliers | Inputs | Process | Outputs | Customers |
|---|---|---|---|---|
| Pt Access | Pt Admission | Admit | Quality Care | Patient |
| Providers | Admission "o" set | Treat | Discharge Plan | Family |
| Bed Control | Room assignment | Discharge | Pain Management | POA |
| Admit RN | Assessment | | Summary of Services | Payors |
| Ancillary Depts. | Tests | | Billing for Services | Providers |
| EVS, RN, Tech | Room set up | | | |
| Biomed Facilities | Plan of Care | | | |
| Pastoral Care | Discharge | | | |
| Dietary | | | | |

Illustration 4.9. SIPOC Example.

### 6. Create charter.

The charter represented in Illustration 4.10 serves as the "contract" between the executive sponsor and the team (see Appendix E for the entire charter template). It identifies the area of focus, the problem statement, team leader, team members, scope, measures, authority of the team, and the limits to their authority. While we want to give the team as much leeway as possible, we are still governed by rules, regulations, financial and FTE resources, capital expenses, etc. Being clear here helps the team stay within appropriate boundaries. If the charter is done well, then the team should have no problems creating countermeasures that will be approved by the sponsor.

If the charter is done right, success is assured, and success looks like a team creating countermeasures that the sponsor will approve. If the team does not succeed, then the fault lies squarely in the lap of the sponsor for not chartering well. The format is not important, but the content is.

116

## Improvement Team Charter  DRAFT

| Title of Project: | SAH CPE MultiWeek Improvement on Inpatient Patient Flow | File name pre fix: G:\ Operational Excellence, Clinical and Process Excellence Approach\SAH CPE\ SAH CPE Charter02-25 .docx |
|---|---|---|
| Department: | ED and Inpatient areas at St. Anthony | |
| **Process Boundaries** | | |
| Issue(s): | provider/community. | |
| Overall Goal(s)[1]: | **Improve the process of delivering care to core medical inpatients** as measured by: Reduction in cost per discharge; Improvement of perfect care scores for MI, HF and Pneumonia; Reduction of in patient discharge process lead time; approach to a primary care team and discharged patient's needs for continuing care. | |
| Criteria for Success | Streamlined process meeting national benchmarks for LOS based on DRGs while maintaining perfect scores for MI and pneumonia. Meet best practice benchmark for HF by 4 quarter 2014. | |
| First Step: | Decision to admit to inpatient or OBS | |
| Last Step: | Disposition with handoff from hospital to comm unity level of care (PCP, SNIF, receiving hospital, etc). | |
| Includes: | All Medical Inpatients | |
| Excludes: | ?Surgical Patients? | |
| Potential Barriers | Time resources, regional resources, Community Resources | |
| Non- negotiable: | Solve the problem with resources available. | |

[1] SMART goals: Specific, Measurable, Action oriented, Relevant to the problem, and time bound

Illustration 4.10. Example Charter.

*In fact, in the hundreds of teams I have facilitated, only two times did the team's countermeasures not get approved. Once was because one of the team members chose to ignore a non-negotiable item in the charter that stated no additional staff may be hired. His recommendation, separate from the rest of the team, was to hire more staff. The sponsor said no.*

*The second time, the sponsor was not up front about what she wanted, as expressed in the charter. She was looking for the team to guess at the solution she already had in her head. Of course, the team did not guess correctly. It is acceptable if a manager or executive already knows the solution or wants to set tight boundaries. You can use a change management method to implement your idea, but don't create a team only to leave them guessing. Let's not play games with people's time. Everyone is too busy for that.*

**7. Conduct team leader training** (5 days). Required for team leader.

This class is predicated on the belief that you want to shift managers from an autocratic/dictatorial leadership style toward a more participative and engaging style. We call this a "facilitative leadership" style. The organizing principle of the facilitative leadership style is that we recognize and honor the skills, knowledge and experience of those who do the work every day: frontline staff.

Often, managers are told to be more facilitative, but are infrequently taught the skills they will need to facilitate effectively. I suggest a course that is five days long, light on lecture, and heavy on practice. This provides both the training and the application of those skills. Furthermore, it takes time for classmates to get comfortable with each other, to take more learning risks, and to strengthen their bonds with one another.

Below are the topics covered each day, with an example of the emphasis and time we put on each element of training. Most of these are common topics for any leadership development professional or Lean advisor. The main topics covered in the facilitator class were:

- Segment 1 (4 hours): Developing a meeting agenda; roles of team leader and members; team dynamics; use of flipcharts, post-its, and markers in meetings.
- Segment 2 (4 hours): Change management with a primary use of Six Sources of Influence.
- Segment 3 (24 hours): Problem solving; training and application of a one-day group/team problem solving method; theory and application of facilitation skills.
- Segment 4 (8 hours): Foundational training taught in the context of an inpatient simulation (explained below).

8. **Conduct foundational training** (8 hours). Required for team members and leaders.

The foundational training is actually Segment 4, and the fifth day, of the facilitator training mentioned above for leaders. We take class members through an inpatient simulation that allows everyone to experience the concepts we are teaching, concepts that they will use during the extended event. It also provides team leaders with an opportunity to coach their team through the tools they will be using.

The basic scenario of the inpatient simulation is that we have several patients being admitted into the process. The patients take the form of a card with patient information and symptoms on them. Each patient has particular LOS requirements and diagnostic services to be overseen by physicians, nurses, and technicians, and each patient will also require the use of certain clinical supplies. Every minute in the simulation represents an hour, and each "round" of the exercise represents 12 hours of the RN's shift.

We repeated the simulated 12-hour shifts several times. In between each shift, participants were taught Lean concepts (such as one-piece flow, continuous flow, Kanbans, just in time, etc.) that they were then expected to apply during the next 12-hour shift. This also reinforces the iterative nature of PDCA through several patient flow process improvement cycles to meet the pre-determined quality, cost, delivery, safety, and morale goals. These can seem completely unattainable at first, but are always achieved by the end of the day.

*I have observed firsthand the difference between those who have been trained and those who have not. Once, I was standing at the end of a partition that separated two rooms and two teams. The leader with training led with confidence and purpose. The one without training simply could not fathom what they needed to do next or how to do it. While this may seem obvious to most of us, for some reason, managers believe they don't need the training, until they don't get it and are lost, confused, and frustrated at not being able to lead their team effectively.*

## B. Team Work

### 1. Typical Week/Meetings

There are five types of meetings that occur during the extended event, as shown in Illustration 4.11. Starting the week, in this case on Tuesday, the first type of meeting is weekly training. Usually, the training simply starts the all-day team meeting by providing an in-depth exploration of the tools and principles the team will be using that day. Some organizations do this as a separate meeting so that they can invite other department staff to learn as well.

The second type of meeting is the team doing the improvement work itself. Team members will meet once a week for an entire day. The time between these weekly meetings can be used to have team members inform others of their progress, test their countermeasures, and gather input. This is described in more detail below.

Extended Event Typical Weekly Calendar

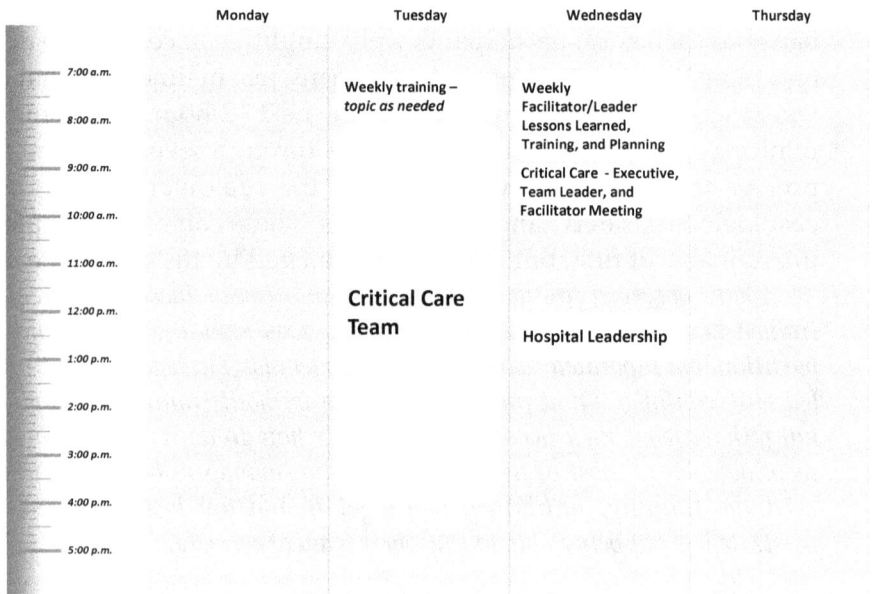

| | Monday | Tuesday | Wednesday | Thursday |
|---|---|---|---|---|
| 7:00 a.m. | | | | |
| 8:00 a.m. | | Weekly training – topic as needed | Weekly Facilitator/Leader Lessons Learned, Training, and Planning | |
| 9:00 a.m. | | | Critical Care - Executive, Team Leader, and Facilitator Meeting | |
| 10:00 a.m. | | | | |
| 11:00 a.m. | | | | |
| 12:00 p.m. | | **Critical Care Team** | | |
| 1:00 p.m. | | | **Hospital Leadership** | |
| 2:00 p.m. | | | | |
| 3:00 p.m. | | | | |
| 4:00 p.m. | | | | |
| 5:00 p.m. | | | | |

Illustration 4.11. Typical Extended Event Weekly Meeting Calendar.

Some of the topics we cover in training are more hands-on, and include patient care stream and process-mapping, analyzing and reducing variability, root cause problem solving, standard work, metrics, and measurements. We also cover more organizational

120

concepts like creating a performance-driven culture, influencing and keeping staff engaged, sustaining change management, giving feedback, and coaching.

The third type of meeting is with the facilitator and team leader to develop the agenda for the next week's team meeting and to coach and train the team leader, as necessary. Frequently, training can be used to prepare the leader, instead of the facilitator, to conduct the training session the following week. The purpose of this kind of meeting is to instill the manager with more confidence as they lead their teams, and also to reinforce the leadership role they will have through the duration of the 13 weeks and after.

The fourth type of meeting involves the executive sponsor (the president or CEO of the hospital), the team leader, and the facilitator. This is an opportunity to keep the executives informed of the team's progress, to discuss the hospital deployment plan and its progress, and to discuss any roadblocks the team is experiencing that need executive attention.

The fifth type of meeting is actually the team facilitator joining the executive's leadership meeting. This enables the facilitator to remain engaged with leadership, to get a feel for any issues that might affect the team, to help prioritize future work, and to meet informally with managers to build relationships.

## 2. Extended Event 13-Week Schedule and Topics

The extended event 13-week schedule is very similar to many Kaizen event agendas that I, and probably some of you, too, have done. The difference is that the extended event "agenda" is spread out over time to allow the work of the team to unfold. Therefore, the agenda creates ongoing opportunities for members to communicate team status and activities to department personnel who are not on the team. It provides an opportunity to gather input from peers and to test run the countermeasures that the team is developing. At this time, hospital leadership should be publicizing the team's status and steps to the rest of the hospital to inform them and garner support for team activities. It is also an opportunity to create, implement, and train staff on the Daily Management Board and huddles.

Illustration 4.12 reflects a typical extended event 13-week schedule for team meetings and the concurrent development of the Daily Management Board (DMB). The evolution of the DMB from project support to clear, operational focus is a natural offshoot of the extended event. The reason is that all of the content for the DMB is being generated during the event meetings. Developing the DMB requires only that the content be posted into the appropriate section.

For those familiar with Kaizen events, you will see that much of the content and actions are the same. Again, two of the biggest differences are the space between team meetings and the capacity to interact with non-team members to do more aggressive testing.

As the third column of Illustration 4.12 shows, building the operational Daily Management Board can begin almost immediately using the topic of safety. Some form of safety information should already be present if the hospital and departments are doing safety huddles. Departmental safety information should be posted from the outset so you can start having the department staff congregate at the DMB for the safety huddle. As you add more data and elements to the DMB, you deepen the conversation with the workgroup, and this keeps them apprised of the team's progress and generates feedback from staff.

## Extended Event 13 Week Plan

| Wk | Topic | Equivalent DMB Element | Training Topics |
|---|---|---|---|
| | Extended Event 13 Week Schedule | | |
| 1 | Kickoff/Charter & SIPOC, Patient Care Value Stream/Process Mapping | Departmental Safety First Cross | Patient Care Stream and Process Mapping |
| 2 | Develop Process Analysis Measures | Trend charts and graphs | Root Cause Problem Solving |
| 3 | Process Analysis Root Cause Analysis | Trend charts and graphs | Metrics & Measurements |
| 4 | Identify and Prioritize Improvement Opportunities Develop or Confirm Progress and Outcome Measures | Improvement opportunities | Analyzing and Reducing Variability |
| 5 | Design Future State (To-Be") Process Design and Draft Standard Work Prepare for Midpoint Report Out | Standard Work Improvement opportunities | Standard Work |
| 6 | Midpoint Report Out to Executives, Managers, Affected Departments | | |
| 6 | Test/Revise Future State Process Design | Standard Work Process Change Alerts Improvement opportunities | Creating a Performance – driven Culture |
| 7 | Test/Revise Future State Process Design | Standard Work Process Change Alerts Improvement opportunities | Influencing, Engagement and Change Management |
| 8 | Test/Revise Future State Process Design | Improvement opportunities on Plan side | Clinical pathways and order sets |
| 9-11 | Test/Revise Future State Process Design | | Sustain, Evidence-based practice, Feedback and Coaching |
| 12 | Finalize and Sustain Implementation Plan Prepare for Final Report Out | | |
| 13 | Conduct Final Report Out | | |

Illustration 4.12. Extended Event 13-Week Schedule.

### 3. Extended Event Tools

Several critical tools that we used during the 13 weeks are discussed below:

#### a. Process Flow Diagram

The first was the process flow diagram. We used this tool to focus on patients and their experience. Then, we identified the process issues and problems using the Kaizen bursts (Illustration 4.13).

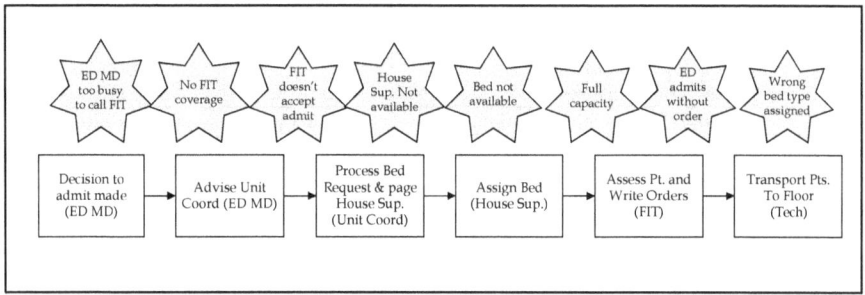

Illustration 4.13. Process Flow Diagram with Kaizen Bursts.

#### b. Four-Step Problem Solving

Once we had identified the issues and selected which ones we would work on, we used a variation of the A3 tool to do root cause analysis and problem solving (Illustration 4.14). Our process was divided into four stages. We first gathered data on the issue, then did the root cause analysis on it using either the fishbone diagram or "5 Whys". Thirdly, we prioritized, when necessary, the order in which we would solve the problems at hand, and then, finally, we came up with countermeasures and action plans to implement them.

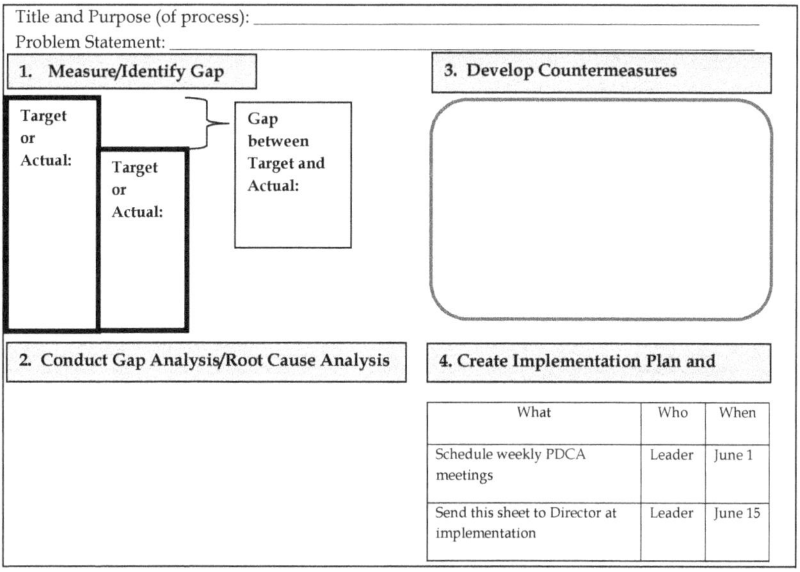

| Title and Purpose (of process): _____ |
| Problem Statement: _____ |

| 1. Measure/Identify Gap | | 3. Develop Countermeasures |
| --- | --- | --- |

Target or Actual:  Target or Actual:  Gap between Target and Actual:

| 2. Conduct Gap Analysis/Root Cause Analysis | 4. Create Implementation Plan and |
| --- | --- |

| What | Who | When |
| --- | --- | --- |
| Schedule weekly PDCA meetings | Leader | June 1 |
| Send this sheet to Director at implementation | Leader | June 15 |

Illustration 4.14. Four-Step Problem Solving Tool.

c.  Standard Work

Standard work is critical to success.  As we know from our discussion of Lean so far and the discussion of standard work in Chapter 3, we are looking for standard, stable, reliable and predictable processes – and standard work is the key to attaining this state.

d.  Daily Management Board

The Daily Management Board (DMB), can be started almost immediately at the beginning of the 13 weeks. Use a shadow board (Illustration 4.15) that reflects all of the items that will eventually fill out the operational DMB. By putting up the shadow board, staff will start to ask questions.  It will be a good opportunity to discuss the DMB and the work the team is doing or will do.  That information

125

will begin to appear on the shadow board, giving everyone access to the team's work.

## Dashboard – Where are we now?

| Customer | Finance | Processes | People |
|---|---|---|---|
| Safety First Calendar - Patients | Productivity | ALOS | Safety First Calendar – Staff |
| Safety Alerts | Revenue | Time to Admit | Training |
| Complaints | Budget | Time to Discharge | Turnover |

## Plans - What Will We Do?

| What | Who | When |
|---|---|---|
|  |  |  |

| Standard Work Sheets | Standard Work Reviews |
|---|---|
|  | Process Changes |

Illustration 4.15. Daily Management Board Template.

**4. Report Outs**

Mid and final report outs should include as many stakeholders as possible, including executives and people affected by the project, and hold the report outs in a conference room or small auditorium. Doing this serves a few purposes. It lets hospital staff know what is about to happen and why. It is a good way to help nudge the culture by showing others what is being done and setting the expectation for them to support the initiative. And, since we are spending a lot of resources on extended events, we want to ensure that leadership sees they are getting their money's worth.

C. Post-Extended Event Activities

At this point, the easy work has now concluded. The attention needs to shift to implementing and sustaining the work your teams have put in. This requires tenacity and discipline, which is what makes the previous work easy, relative to what is to follow. Most projects fail because they do not consistently and emphatically attend to the next steps. In the 30 years that I have been doing this work, I have been asked many times what can be done to succeed and why improvement efforts fail—giving it that "flavor-of-the-month" feel. It is simple: in some form or another, you must check-and-adjust, check-and-adjust, check-and-adjust, from now on. As soon as you stop, it's over. That simple.

**1. Use PDCA (Plan, Do, Check, Adjust).**

Before the 13 weeks is over, be sure to schedule weekly one-hour team meetings to discuss how the implementation process is going, any adjustments to the plans that need to be made, the standard work or other countermeasures, and the transition to the sustain stage. I have found that everything up to this point was easy compared to sustaining the gains. The only effective method I know for successful implementation and sustain is to meet on a consistent basis to work through issues and reinforce changes.

### 2. Conduct huddles at Daily Management Board.

Another mechanism for sustaining the gains and continuing the culture of continuous improvement is using the Daily Management Board. This has to be incorporated into the daily routine and seen as a natural part of work, not merely an addition to it.

### 3. Hold additional workshops.

Even after 13 weeks, not all of the issues will have been resolved. They might require any number of actions, activities, workshops, JDIs, etc., to continue improving patient care, process flow and service delivery.

### 4. Conduct governing meetings.

Like the PDCA meetings and Daily Management Boards, it is critical that this work be incorporated into the operations meetings of executives and managers. Measures and goals should be frequently and consistently reviewed for progress. Executives should be monitoring implementation and should be ready to help support staff when they hit roadblocks or resistance. If the executives cannot find the time to do this, then I would recommend not attempting this work in the first place.

With all of the distractions and competing priorities, this is the hardest part for executives to do consistently, and requires the most discipline. However, this is where success will be realized: top leadership staying abreast of the work they chartered and supporting it at all levels to meet the goals that have been set out.

### Final Thoughts

I was initially skeptical about the efficacy of extended event as we were first creating and implementing it, thinking that it was just a glorified Kaizen event. However, the amount of improvement that could be accomplished, the commitment that was rallied as the team progressed, the cultural shifts that became apparent, the sense of empowerment, and, of course, the results all added up to a much more significant impact than just meeting for a week. It is hard work preparing for and conducting this prolonged event, but I have found it far superior to other approaches for making the kind of leveraged difference we wanted.

The major advantage of this approach is being able to work on a large complex process with more time and resources, while allowing team members to check in with peers and managers and to get action items done in between team meetings. While we did extensive training before starting the team meetings, we also used the time between weekly team meetings to provide training on concepts more directly related to the team's needs.

Divided into three major phases (preparation, weekly meetings, and post-meeting activities), this approach both requires and reinforces daily integration of Lean into everyday work. By doing so, we start to shift the culture of the organization toward daily, versus episodic, improvement, as the journey unfolds.

Integrating measurement extensively into the work also becomes less problematic. The work done ahead of time and the refinement of the measures during the extended time frame makes measuring more real and meaningful for frontline staff. One team member described the use of measurement as "myth-busting" because they stopped using anecdotal stories and started objectively capturing what was actually happening.

While not applicable to every situation, the extended event approach is especially useful for complex processes found in the emergency department and inpatient departments.

# Chapter 5 — Using 5S for Early Frontline Engagement

### Starting with 5S (Sort, Simplify, Sweep, Standardize and Sustain)

As soon as leaders decide to embark on the Lean journey, most want to achieve results as quickly as possible. Let's face it: once we decide on a course of action, we want results yesterday! That makes sense; resources in many guises will be spent establishing and implementing a new Lean culture. Strong commitments of time, money, and people are all required, and, justifiably, a return on that investment is necessary. This is not, of course, just about money. We want to engage frontline staff as soon as possible because they perform the work and provide the care. Therefore, they are in the best position to know how to improve the care of patients.

But herein lies the conundrum. The Lean journey is not a quick fix. It requires the acquisition of new skills and discipline. Not unlike achieving a healthy lifestyle, it takes time to change culture and habits. Achieving a healthy lifestyle that ultimately results in weight loss is different than going on a diet to achieve quick weight loss irrespective of its health consequences. However, the right change in lifestyle (such as cutting out sugars or alcohol) can sometimes result in dramatic reductions in weight rather quickly. There are too many variables, too many interdependencies, too many people, and too many broken sub-processes and systems for this to result in a quick fix.

How do you improve efficiency and effectiveness in your organization? How do you visually and functionally impact the workplace while also reducing costs? In my experience, the fastest way to engage leaders and staff at all levels of the organization is to implement 5S. It is a quick and useful empowerment approach, but 5S can also be a superficial one if not soon parlayed into more fundamental process improvement efforts to enculturate the principles and values of Lean. While some organizations have viewed 5S as simply housekeeping, if done well, this activity can result in changes to workflow patterns that significantly improve the efficiency and effectiveness of the organization.

This chapter discusses how we implemented 5S, starting with the Critical Care unit of one of our hospitals. As I have mentioned, I recommend that you think about where your own leverage area might be and consider how you would use 5S; everything related here is essentially a recommendation on how to use this tool to your greatest advantage. In our case, it really made a difference in getting nurses, doctors, and others on board with Lean. Because of external circumstances, we admittedly stumbled at first as to where and how to use 5S, though we quickly used it to its full potential. I hope you'll see the value of what we did, and take advantage of our learning curve.

The best part about implementing 5S is that it is so easy to understand, teach, use, and replicate. And the impact is virtually immediate. It should be noted, though, that the biggest logistical challenge in doing 5S is creating and implementing standard work areas across different departments or an entire system, as in a multi-hospital network. As will be described in detail below, if the organization wants to create, for example, a standard supply room structure across the clinical departments, this will take more work than simply organizing one department's supply room or one operating room.

## Our 5S Approach

The description of our experience using 5S in the hospital system is divided into two sections. The first section (Phase 1) describes the application of 5S in the Critical Care Unit in one hospital. Included are descriptions of the materials, such as charters, agendas, and training materials necessary to use 5S.

The second section (Phase 2) takes the application of 5S across the entire system, to attain the same type of results but on a larger scale. The description includes necessary structures and actions to support it. The work that we did in one Critical Care unit eventually expanded to engage 22 clinical units in three hospitals.

We chose clinical supplies and equipment to apply 5S to for a few reasons. The first reason was that one of the nurses in Critical Care was studying 5S as a part of her Master's degree and wanted to apply it to her area, so this was a natural place to start. However, it was also a serendipitous moment for all of us. We did not realize in the initial months of her project that this was precisely our hoped-for "tipping point" that would catalyze the transformation of our organization.

The second reason is that 5S is done in a localized geographical area, unlike a process that goes across departments and functions, so it was easily contained within a given physical space. Thirdly, a central supply room was the one area common to all clinical departments. And, finally, not being able to find supplies and equipment is one of the biggest complaints from nurses. In fact, a survey we did of over 100 managers and staff in both the clinical and ancillary departments identified supplies and equipment as their number one concern.

## Phase 1 — Critical Care Unit

The Lean program manager created a 15-minute video on 5S to prepare the team and department for the event. The video described what 5S is and highlighted the value of doing it. It also laid out the agenda for the "event" day, and outlined how to implement 5S. We found it easier to have a standard and easily accessible means to tell everyone what 5S was.

The Critical Care 5S team consisted of employees from the Critical Care department, representing both shifts and including nurses as well as care assistants. The nurse in Critical Care who was working on her Master's degree with this project served as the Unit Champion (UC) and facilitated this 5S team.

The Lean Program Manager met with the Unit Champion and her manager to write the 5S charter. Although the Lean Program Manager attended the first 5S event to provide coaching, the main emphasis was on the department's ability to execute 5S events after the first one without the Lean Program Manager or other facilitators present.

We used the 5S workshop agenda below (Illustration 5.1). Oftentimes, managers and staff would be resistant to the fact this event took an entire day. After all, how hard is it to clean a room and reorganize it? We heavily emphasized to department managers and staff that the first time they did 5S required them to follow the process in this exact sequence, and that it would be an eight-hour event, because clearly it was about more than just cleaning the supply room.

We explained that a 5S event is about group discussion and decision-making in order to reach a consensus on how the area should be organized. This was foreign to many people who were used to reorganizing an area on their own and then failed to understand why no one else was on the same page. We were intentional that the first time through 5S, everyone should remain in lockstep through the whole process. There were frequent requests

| Time | Mins | Task/Content | Notes/Materials |
|---|---|---|---|
| | 30-45 | Prior to the 5S day, **show 5S video** to as many people in organization as possible<br>○ Review handouts | |
| 8:00 | 30 | **Plan for the day**<br>○ Review goals and agenda for the day<br>○ Introductions<br>○ Review definitions<br>○ TAKE PRE-PHOTOS | Conference room<br>Flip charts & markers |
| 8:30 | 120 | **Red Tag Strategy (Sort)**<br>○ Establish locations for staging items for needed/not needed<br>○ Establish teams for different areas if appropriate<br>**Sort &Red-Tag as a Team**<br>○ Sort items as they are removed from space<br>○ Red-tag (or use yellow post-its) unneeded items<br>○ Ask: "Who uses this?" "How often?" "What do we do with it?" "Consensus?"<br>○ Place in designated locations | Red tags or yellow post-its |
| 10:30 | 30 | **Clean Rooms**<br>○ Clean out rooms – vacuum, mop, dust, etc. | Cleaning materials available |
| 11:00 | 60 | **Re-huddle to redesign room layout (Simplify)**<br>○ Identify design principles (e.g. frequency of use, ergonomics: golden triangle and back)<br>○ Determine if shelves need to be reconfigured<br>○ Redesign the space, as needed<br>○ Use temporary signs to establish locations<br>○ Apply tape to establish boundaries | Meeting room<br>Card stock for temporary signs<br>Tape |
| 12:00 | 30 | **LUNCH** | |
| 12:30 | 3.5 hours | **Move needed items to location (Sweep)**<br>○ Move equipment & supplies back into spaces<br>○ Create labels and other forms of visual controls (visual sweep)<br>○ Develop a map of the space<br>○ TAKE POST-PHOTOS | |
| 4:00 | 30 | **Action planning & final celebration**<br>○ Identify next steps and who will do what<br>○ Determine how to get feedback from staff<br>○ Identify (fun) ways to get everyone to follow new standards **(Standardize)**<br>○ Meet weekly to "check and adjust" until not necessary **(Sustain)**<br>○ Discuss consequences for not following standards<br>○ Celebrate! | Meeting Room<br>Flipchart |
| 4:30 | | **Adjourn** | |

Illustration 5.1. One Day 5S Example Agenda.

to divide the team in half and to do two areas at once. I rarely acquiesced because I wanted a whole team effort the first time for the reasons I mentioned above. Plus, the process itself was carefully designed to get them to the same place at the end of the day.

If staff wanted to shorten the length of time to do another 5S event later, which was fine, as long as they stayed with the same sequence of events. Notice, by the way, that a 5S workshop actually covers only the first four S's. It is the hard, ongoing work of sustain/self-discipline that constitutes the last S.

Preparation and Training

Everyone in the Critical Care department was required to view the 5S video. The reasons for viewing the video were twofold:

- To ensure that everyone knew what was about to happen so that they could support (or at least not interfere with) the 5S effort.
- To train those participating in the 5S effort on what would be expected of them.

The Unit Champion held several meetings in preparation for the event day. This day became known alternatively as the "5S event day" and the "Sort day." During these prep meetings, the group decided on a color-coded supply system categorized by the function of the actual supply item (Illustration 5.2). All medical and patient care supplies were then categorized into the five colors based on how they were used. Colored bins were purchased in several sizes to match the category colors. Wire shelving for the bins was already installed in the supply areas, so cost was minimal. If you already have bins and they are of the same color, colored tape can be used instead of purchasing colored bins. Just make sure the stock bar code remains visible.

The color-coded system was a visually distinctive feature, and was structured so that like-items were stocked next to like-items. For example, all bathing products were stocked in the same location in tan bins. All items used in point of care testing were grouped in red bins. This included items such as lab tubes, culturettes, cotton balls,

135

and lancets. All the color-coded bins were then labeled with clear, large tape labels. This enabled staff to easily identify the product they were searching for, and also helped the person stocking the supplies to easily discern where to appropriately place the products.

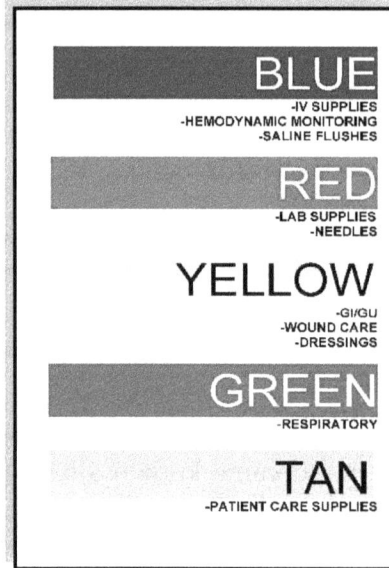

Illustration 5.2. Color-Coded Categories for Supply Items.

On the 5S event day, the Critical Care 5S team, as well as ancillary departments such as respiratory therapists and materials management staff, physically categorized thousands of supplies into the color-coded system. Stocking levels were adjusted, and items most frequently used were placed at shelf levels that did not require reaching or bending. A very large supply room was converted on that one day. After the 5S event day, posters were printed, laminated, and placed in the supply areas to reinforce the new color system. This served as a reference for anyone entering the supply room to obtain a product.

To get input from staff, we placed flip chart paper on the wall asking staff for feedback. We did this because we wanted to know whether supplies had accidentally dropped off our profiles; if our stocking levels were adequate; if the color itemizing was logical and accurate; and because we wanted to obtain any other feedback staff was willing to share with us.

This project was meant to improve staff workflow and satisfaction regarding finding supplies, and we wanted all staff to feel as if they had a voice in the final design. This feedback was then brought back to the unit's 5S team to evaluate and determine what adjustments were necessary. Illustration 5.3 shows how one of Critical Care's supply rooms looked after the 5S event day.

As a part of the fifth S, "sustain," a PowerPoint presentation was developed to describe the 5S process and how Critical Care transformed its supply areas. This presentation was first provided to all of the current nursing staff to educate them on the new system. Then, it was given to newly hired employees in Critical Care as part of their on-boarding.

Once Critical Care staff transformed their supply areas, they presented the unit's experience to the sponsor (in this case, the department director) during a project "report out" in one of the hospital conference rooms. Having photos enabled the sponsors of the project to see first-hand the transformation of the supply areas. It also meant that the experience could be shared and celebrated by those attending the meeting. Note: had we to do this presentation with the director again, it would have been at the

Illustration 5.3. Critical Care Supply Room Using New Color-Coded System.

*gemba*, not a conference room. Recall from Chapter 1 that *gemba* means to go to the actual place, to see the actual process, and talk to the actual team members.

### Phase 2 — Expansion to Other Inpatient Units

Then something really fascinating started to happen. The Critical Care unit was on the sixth floor of a 12 floor hospital building. It turns out that the nurses on the adjacent floors found that it was faster to go to the sixth floor to get supplies than their own supply rooms! That meant the sixth floor was supplying an additional two floors, which, while it was assuring to know what an efficient job the sixth floor had done, was not an acceptable workflow to budget-conscious managers.

The adjoining department managers met and insisted that 1) no one go to the sixth floor for supplies who did not work there, and 2) that they replicate the 5S activity in their own departments. Expansion was born!

Since word of our success had gotten out to all of the clinical areas, we recommended to leadership that we implement this process across the three system hospitals. So, after using Critical Care as our "accidental" trial area to refine the 5S approach, we were ready to use 5S to expand the reorganization and standardization of the supply rooms system-wide. The expansion included three hospitals in the Puget Sound area. The first hospital had 110 beds, the second had 320 beds, and the third 106 beds. Collectively, this system consisted of 22 units (including the EDs and pharmacies) and Materials Management, all of which would reorganize to this standardized structure of supplies and equipment. The initial color-code system for the supply rooms was developed by the Critical Care 5S group. It was then presented to representatives of the entire system's clinical areas for their endorsement. Minor changes were made to items in the categories, and then it was adopted.

With the color-coded system clearly defined, an instructional video on hand, lessons learned from the initial trial, and the direction from leadership to conduct 5S in each inpatient care unit, the next step was deciding when each of the 22 units would hold their own 5S events.

To ensure that a project of this magnitude would be sponsored well and enhance our chances of success, we created a governing structure with defined level-appropriate roles and responsibilities, and then created a schematic to help participants visualize the cascading nature of the plan (Illustration 5.4). Since sustaining the outcomes of process improvement efforts has long been our Achilles heel, we created a structure to support 5S implementation *and* sustain the results.

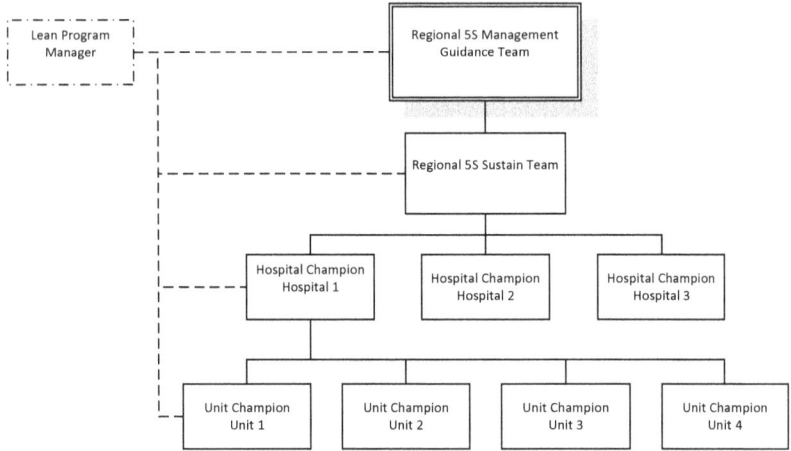

Illustration 5.4. Regional 5S Governing Structure.

The **Regional 5S Management Guidance Team** (5S MGT) consisted of the clinical managers, directors, COOs, and the executive sponsor of the Regional 5S project. They met with the Regional 5S Sustain Team to ensure standardization across the hospitals, to resolve cross-functional authority issues, and to provide requested guidance to the units. In order to identify what the major factors for progress and hindrance would be, this team was established before the work of Critical Care had actually started.

The **Regional 5S Sustain Team** consisted of the Hospital Champions (HCs) and Unit Champions (UCs), and was led by the Lean program manager. Its purpose was to discuss and resolve region-wide issues, to share lessons learned, to advise the 5S MGT on how to ensure successful implementation, and to learn more about 5S and visual control to advance the use of this Lean method. For example, at one meeting, we discussed the fact that there were units using department-specific supplies, such as peritoneal dialysis care. Instead of separating dozens of items for this diagnosis into five different colored bins, the group decided that these types of supplies could be grouped together and placed into orange bins. This allowed for separation from the main supply chain, but logically grouped the supplies together so hospital staff could find them easily.

The **Hospital Champions** were, in this case, the keepers of the color-coded categories. They were responsible for ensuring that the clinical units kept the supply items in the appropriate categories. They acted as advisors to the Unit Champions and their respective nursing units, and they also advised the Lean program manager before, during, and after the 5S events. Typically, an experienced Supply Coordinator acted as the HC.

The **Unit Champions**, along with their managers, were responsible for ensuring that everyone in the department viewed the 5S video prior to the 5S event day. They helped select team members and oversee the planning and logistics of the 5S event, and then led the team through the 5S event day. The UCs were among the most significant players, as they were the primary contact for the HCs and Lean program manager before, during, and after the 5S event. Typically, this was also a Supply Coordinator, some of whom did double duty as the HC.

The **5S Team Members** would do the planning, sorting, simplifying, and sweeping on the day of the event. This team consisted of representatives from as many areas, functions, and specialties in the unit as possible. Whoever was affected by the change was encouraged to participate on the team. The Central Supply Representatives (CSRs) were invited to help with planning and implementation on the 5S event day; they helped relabel the supply bins and adjust the PAR (inventory) level for items in our computerized supply system.

## Results

Overall, we were pleased with the success of the project. Although it took some time for people to get used to the new shelf location of supplies, this was far outweighed by having everything well organized and easier to find.

Illustration 5.5. OR Suture Cabinet Before and After 5S.

Change was difficult to accept for some staff, but after they learned the new system, they did find it to be more useful and better organized. We also learned that new staff adapted more quickly to the supply system than existing staff, as they did not necessarily have to 'unlearn' and then 'relearn' the process. Illustration 5.5 shows the before and after pictures from one of the units that has implemented 5S.

We quantified the before- and after-state of the supply rooms and staff attitudes by surveying the staff. Although we did not consider the surveys to be a "scientific" study per se, they did give a good indication of the positive impact that doing 5S has had on the nursing staff. All units that conducted 5S were surveyed.

The survey results in Illustration 5.6 answer the question "How much time did you spend on your 8-hour shift looking for supplies?" While we also gathered objective data, represented in Illustration 5.9, we wanted to determine if gathering supplies *felt* faster and, if it did, how much faster it felt. In other words, we wanted to reinforce their subjective experience of the new organization feeling faster and more accessible. The survey results indicated that gathering

142

supplies took significantly less time than before, with the average time dropping from 32.44 minutes per shift to 12.89 minutes.

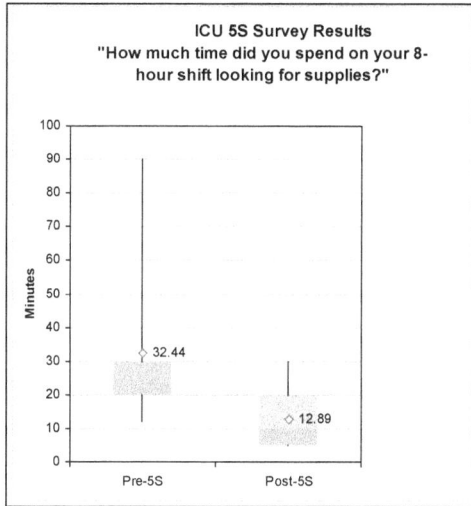

Illustration 5.6. Answers to Survey Question.

The next two surveys were also meant to gather staff's subjective experience of how the supplies were reorganized (Illustrations 5.7 and 5.8). The overall satisfaction score changed dramatically from 'hard' in the Pre-5S conditions to 'easy' in the Post-5S conditions. Likewise, the same was true for locating supplies.

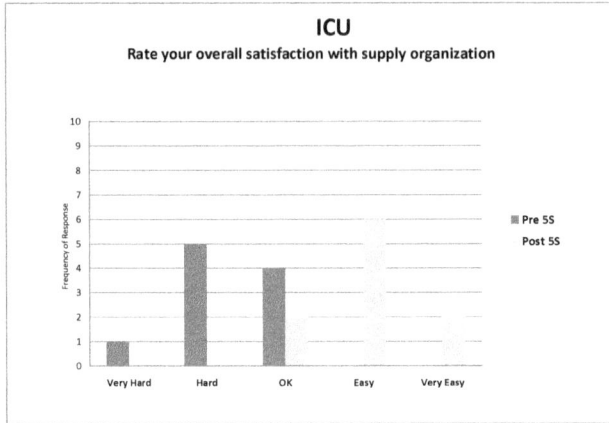

Illustration 5.7. Survey Response Rating Overall Satisfaction.

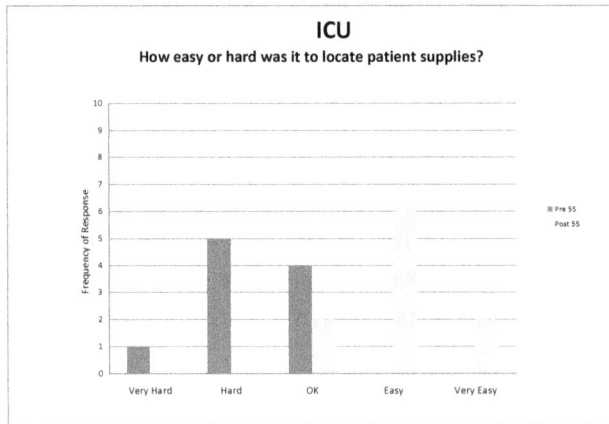

Illustration 5.8. Survey Response Rating How Easy or Hard It Was to Locate Patient Supplies.

The Math

We wanted to quantify the savings, too. We had timed several nurses at finding supplies before doing 5S. To account for familiarity with their own supplies, each nurse was required to go to a different

144

unit with which they weren't familiar. We wanted to be able to measure lost time for new nurses, agency, and floaters, because when nurses run out of supplies in their own unit, they don't hesitate to go to other units, which are typically organized differently. We wanted to obviate that practice by having all supplies organized the same way and always stocked in time.

Each nurse started at the entrance door to the supply room and was given a list of ten items to find. Each item was given to them one at a time. They were timed from the moment they were given the name of each identified item until they returned to the same door with the item in hand.

Our simple math, shown in Illustration 5.9, reveals that we saved approximately 78% of the time nurses had to search for items.

Near-empty bins would be refilled automatically based on their scheduled stocking time. If a critical item did run out (as evidenced by an empty bin), staff could easily write down the number from the front of the bin, phone the supply department, and expect the supplies to be restocked in a timely manner. PAR would be analyzed for adjustment. If a new procedure was introduced or a new product was requested from a physician, staff could give that feedback to their 5S team so that it could be incorporated into the color-coded system and added to PAR.

This all required extensive involvement and negotiation with the supply department. To ensure uniformity, the process for ordering and introducing new products had to be revised. This would improve delivery and tighten limits on how and when existing and new supplies could be added. Various methods were tried among the departments to create effective reordering systems to ensure no item ran out. Simply having the supply room well organized went a long way to keeping supplies readily available.

| Per Day | Before 5S | After 5S | Difference | Total Number of Hours Saved Per: | |
|---|---|---|---|---|---|
| Average number of items picked per day | 19,161 | 19,161 | NA | Day | 192 |
| Average number of seconds to pick supplies | 46 | 10 | 36 | Week | 1,341 |
| Total number of seconds for items picked | 14,960 | 3,193 | 11,497 | Month | 5,748 |
| Total number of hours for items picked | 245 | 53 | 192 | Year | 69,938 |

Illustration 5.9. Supply Pick Savings Calculations.

During the last Regional 5S Sustain Team meeting, we visited the units at two of the three participating hospitals. Our purpose for the visits was to see how each unit had implemented 5S and do an impromptu survey of what worked and what did not work about using 5S in the supply rooms.

Although everyone was required to use the color-coded categories and to have the right items in the right categories, they were given latitude about how this was done. For example, some units chose to use colored bins for each category, while other units used tape to demarcate the categories (Illustration 5.10).

146

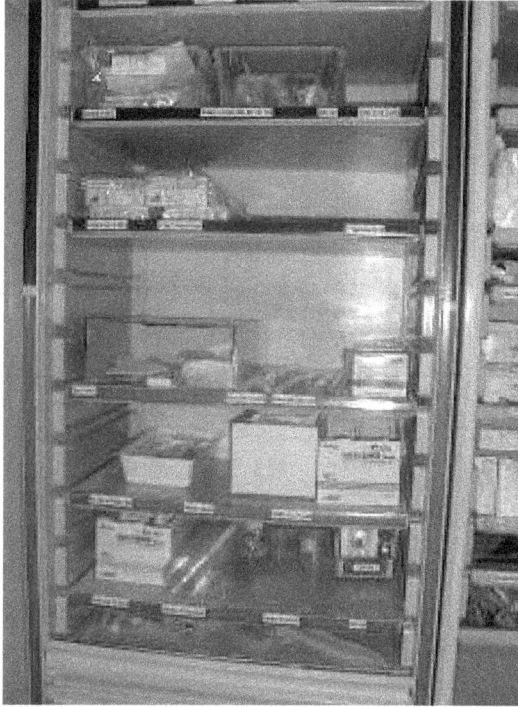

Illustration 5.10. Rehab Supply Locker Using Tape to Demarcate the Categories.

Challenges

The major challenges we faced were ensuring that all the units had the items in their correct respective categories, keeping items at their PAR levels, and integrating new products into the correct color-coded bins. The Hospital Champions and Unit Champions played a significant role in monitoring and ensuring compliance.

In order for 5S to be successful, staff had to learn to trust the new system for stocking supplies. One of the most significant challenges we faced was the staff's tendency to hoard supplies and equipment. Staff were so used to running out of items that they were creating a

147

self-fulfilling prophesy by their own behavior. Staff grabbed handfuls of product and stashed them into secret cabinets or their pockets, or they overfilled their unit's supply carts. This in turn led to increased supply usage and allowed products to expire because they were hidden away.

Lessons Learned

One of the most important lessons we learned was to adopt standards and adapt to circumstances. We had learned a big lesson in first trying to do Lean activities without allowing adequate time to schedule team members for the prep meetings and the event day. Learning from this oversight, we decided to let each unit do 5S at its convenience so that the events would fit into staff work schedules. The only caveat was that it had to be done within the calendar year.

You might decide to be more aggressive in your 5S implementation. However, the scheduling cycle must be honored, otherwise attendance, and, therefore, buy-in, will be weak. We also learned that not all the units were doing the necessary follow-up work on issues that had been raised by staff, such as:

- Inability to see through packaging
- Too many materials in too small a room
- Too many products in bins without dividers
- Need for bigger labels
- Need for timelier stocking of supplies
- Inability to see small supplies behind bigger items
- Linen in supply rooms

We applied PDCA to our experience with each unit. The challenges we experienced reshaped our approach, and, in some instances, caused us to renegotiate roles and responsibilities both on the floor and between the UCs and HCs.

Overall, we were very pleased with the progress we made and the success we achieved. We believed that doing 5S had an immediate and significant positive impact on our clinical units. The success increased the departments' acceptance of the overall Lean applications. This was evidenced by the significant increase in requests for subsequent Lean events.

## Ripple Effect

The culture began to shift as operations experienced new levels of empowerment and began to exercise control of their work environment. The success we achieved opened the door to implanting higher levels of Lean and process improvement methods. Now that we had the attention of nurses, doctors, managers, and staff, it was much easier to introduce more Lean concepts and approaches.

## Summary

This was a story about why and how we did 5S in a clinical department and then expanded it to the rest of the hospital areas. I am hoping that you also saw it as a blueprint both for repeating our successes and learning from our mistakes.

We focused on an area of the hospital that is important to every service provided in a clinical department: the supply room. The Critical Care unit provided us with a small-scale application of 5S so that we could develop methods, standards, and better approaches that were eventually used and adjusted system-wide.

Though the Critical Care unit was an accidental pilot, we saw that the lessons learned and the successes could be replicated in other areas. This resulted in our expanding to other clinical areas and then quickly to the other hospitals.

Critical to our system-wide success was having structures to oversee and manage the activities. This required training a whole cadre of people who would act as unit and hospital focal points; they served as local experts and decision-making representatives to the larger group regarding what should be standardized and what could be unique to each unit.

Ultimately, the staff felt like they finally had control over their supply room and were open to this new sense of empowerment, which led to more Lean activities in various forms beyond 5S.

# Chapter 6 — Operational Excellence Department Structure

## Structure

These improvement efforts require correct placement. While not shown in the diagram (Illustration 6.1), the department should report to the highest level in the organization as possible, preferably to the CEO, COO, or President. If you want this group to have the prestige and credibility of other important support organizations such as QA, HR, and IT, then it needs to be placed at a comparable level. Where the Operational Excellence department is placed will speak volumes to the status with which you hold it and its importance to the business or organization. As my role in the organization grew, the higher I was placed and titled, starting at Project Manager, then Program Manager, then Director, and then, finally, Division Director. By that point, the message was clear to everyone how valued and important this work was viewed by leadership.

Of course, all of these improvement efforts require experienced and knowledgeable people who can facilitate the conversations, methods, and workshops. The skill required to do this is frequently underestimated. A full department will need Lean experts to both do the work and to develop the ability in others. Below are my recommendations for how to structure this group. I have yet to see strong evidence about the ideal ratio of Process Improvement Consultants to the number of staff or hospitals. I know what worked and did not work for me. I am resource-conservative by nature, so I do not recommend putting everyone in place all at once. They will end up sitting around until demand is built.

A word of caution: we have to be careful when a distinct department is created that we aren't sending the message that improvement work is done as a separate addition to regular work. Remember, Lean is all about developing a new culture throughout the entire organization. So, setting up a separate organization means to have a ready group of experts on hand to advise and coach, not do the improvements. Similar role as Quality and HR.

In our case, we started out wrong. We had set up steering committees for selecting projects. These committees were made up of operational/clinical leaders, but were separate from operational meetings. This created a parallel structure to operations that gave the impression that improvement activities were separate from and in addition to the daily work. We later fixed this by eliminating the steering committees and including Lean advisors in the operational meetings to offer guidance.

The role of having an Operational Excellence (OpEx) department is not unlike having a Quality Assurance department or Human Resources department. These departments do not absolve managers and staff from meeting standards and requirements, but rather serve as a focal point of expertise to support managers and staff in meeting those requirements.

At one point my department had four full-time Process Improvement Consultants, one Metric Consultant, and one Administrative Assistant to support five hospitals in five nearby cities. With a combined total of 701 beds (broken down to 25, 80, 106, 124, and 366 beds at each hospital), we frequently struggled to keep up with the work. In the 124-bed hospital, the president moved two of his nurses into Lean Facilitator positions because I could not expand quickly enough to meet his resource demand. We were unable to support the medical group clinics. Later, we expanded more, but never enough for the additional four hospitals that were added, so we had to be selective about who we supported.

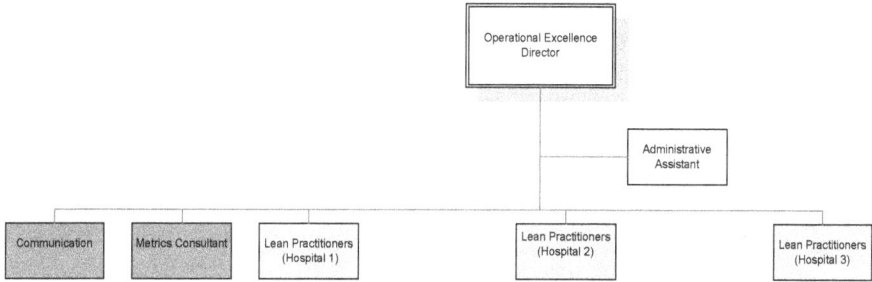

Illustration 6.1. OpEx Structure — Full-Time Permanent Staff.

Director

The first person in a new Operational Excellence department will be the leader of the department and should also be a practitioner — someone who has facilitated teams and taught classes for years or decades. In the beginning, they should actively be setting up the structure of the department and the strategies of improvement efforts (like, for example, following the outlines given in this book) in accordance with the organization's leadership. The Director of Operational Excellence should also be leading teams and classes. There are two practical reasons for this: first, as a resource to doing the work of process improvement; while leading by example and coaching his/her peers in the role of sponsors, and managers and project leads in their roles.

Secondly, an active leader increases credibility and competence of understanding the application and impact of these tools on the organization as a whole. In other words, being too divorced from field operations will result in a misunderstanding of the field and the factors that will drive your organization's success.

Administrative Assistant

153

The second person to be hired is an Administrative Assistant to help keep the calendar, class schedules, workshops, etc., organized and planned out, first for the director, and then for the other Lean practitioners as they come on board. Easily 50% of a practitioner's time can be consumed in the logistics of setting up meetings, training, and workshops.

## Lean Practitioners

The most obvious next group to be hired includes the Lean Practitioners whose primary function is to help identify high leverage areas for improvement. As this group is assembled, it will free up the department head to focus more on strategic and structural development, and relationship building.

One of the most frequently asked questions is how many Lean Practitioners or experts there should be. We had six Lean Practitioners supporting five hospitals (two working at the largest hospital) with a combined total of 701 beds, which breaks down to a ratio of one practitioner for every 116 beds. However, there are so many variables regarding skill level, resource demand, level of implementation and sustainment, and the intensity of shifting to a Lean culture, that I recommend envisioning a large department to meet the demand. That said, it is better to start small at first.

## Metrics Consultant

The fourth addition to this department should be a Metrics Consultant. This person is responsible for measuring baselines before teams start their work, and monitoring progress throughout the improvement period and for a year past the implementation. In addition, they should be teaching managers how to do this work. As mentioned earlier, managers usually do not know how to translate management measures to frontline staff measures. This person can be invaluable for coaching leadership on this.

## Communications

If there is one additional hire that will be especially useful during extended events, it would be a communications person. They will keep the affected hospital and clinical ancillary service departments informed about what is happening and why. In the midst of all the project activity, it is too easy to miss the crucial step of letting staff know about the work that is being done. It is hard for staff to support something they don't know about. This is a classic change management approach of keeping everyone informed of the 'what' and 'why' of the change initiatives.

Lean Facilitators/Lean Fellows

Now we turn to the part-time supplemental support. A great way to embed Lean and process improvement principles into the core of your organization is to use the people *within* the organization. Sometimes called Lean Facilitators or Lean Fellows, they help co-facilitate workshops in addition to their normal job duties (Illustration 6.2). Lean will not work in the long run if it is exclusively dependent on the Lean experts.

Operations managers and staff need to be taught how to be facilitative leaders (versus top-down or autocratic leaders). The amount of time they spend co-facilitating varies depending upon their schedule and the number of projects or workshops. Until the Lean Facilitators gain considerable experience and skill, they will be a resource consumer of your Lean staff, but ultimately, they will help augment your central group at the hospital and local-level. Expect these folks to take 6-8 months of active facilitation to be confident in their skills.

Illustration 6.2 below is notional and is meant to indicate that the number of Lean Facilitators can vary depending on the hospital size. Each facilitator is assigned to a mentor who is responsible for coaching them.

The biggest lesson I've learned over the years of process and service delivery improvement is that Lean must not be perceived as "in addition to" or separate from regular work. It must become part of the fabric of the organization itself. This means transitioning the skills from the experts to into the hands of line personnel.

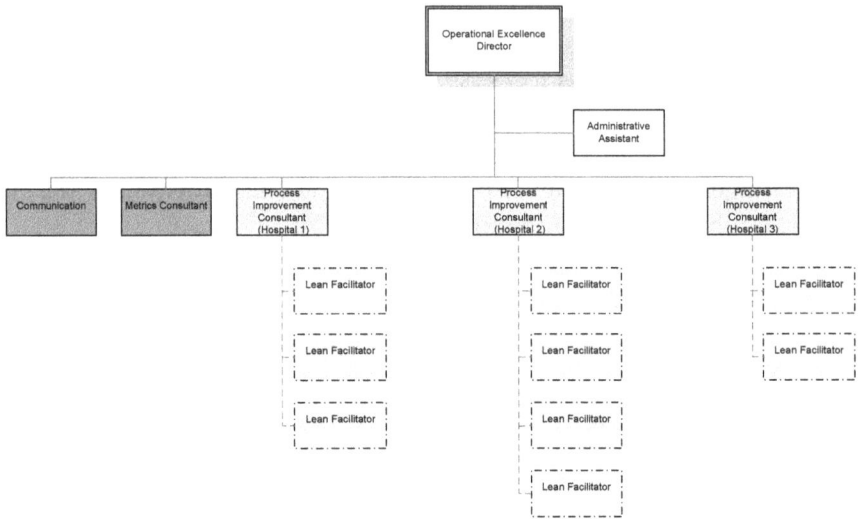

Illustration 6.2. Operational Excellence Department Structure with Addition of Lean Facilitators.

It is a mistake to focus on implementing Lean in a hospital for the sole purpose of cost reduction. Most of this work is culture shift, after all. However, it is not unreasonable to expect a Lean expert to save costs or increase in revenue $3.00 for every $1.00 of salary. In fact, my department as a whole had a target cost savings ratio of 3:1, based on the combined efforts of everyone in the department. I introduced the concept of billable hours to them to place value on their time. This was an indicator of success, but not put in Performance Evaluations as a hard target.

Centralized or Decentralized?

I have experienced both a central Operational Excellence department and one that was decentralized (and sometimes a combination of the two). The advantage of centralization is that it easily keeps everyone aligned around basic philosophies, concepts, tools and methods. The downside of centralization is the possible lack of understanding by central Lean practitioners and consultants of the nuances of the client's organizational issues. Of course, the opposite advantages and disadvantages hold true for a decentralized Operational Excellence department.

There are two major disadvantages of decentralization. First, the training and coaching/mentoring of facilitators is harder to do so that they progress in their understanding and application of Lean concepts, principles, and tools. Secondly, there exists the tendency for decentralized consultants and their clients to become territorial. Instead of working together in a centralized way, it can be easy for a "We got this!" mentality to creep in and take hold. For that reason alone, I have found that having a centralized organization, with consultants embedded in and residing at the client organization, tends to work best. This allows them to develop trust and better working relationships, and allows for more hands-on understanding and rapid responsiveness, without sacrificing the obvious advantages of having everyone on the same philosophical and methodological page.

Summary

This book has laid out the importance of starting with Lean as a mechanism for creating cultural change. That is, shifting to a culture of respect for people and continuous improvement. This always seems easy until we start the journey. Most important in the cultural shift is recognizing that most of what constitutes "Lean" are tools. The tools are important and useful for building a Lean Culture, but they are not the end-state. Hammers help me build, but I'm not enamored with hammers, I just want to build a home. There are thousands of tools I can use, but they ultimately serve the higher purpose.

The success you have on the frontline is dependent upon what happens at the top. Tools such as strategic plans, Balanced Scorecards and Daily Management Boards can help align the organization to provide better quality patient care. But leaders must step up to actively support this endeavor. The literature is replete with examples of success and failure, and the one common denominator to both is the commitment of leaders. One indicator of commitment is whether you as a leader could explain or coach others on Lean principles and tools. If not, then the message is, "This is good stuff, now *you* go do it." Effectively implementing Lean requires modelling and demonstrating the belief system associated with it.

You know this, of course, but the day-to-day distractions of crises, board meetings, making margin, and meeting with regulators frequently makes it difficult to stay the course. I will remind you of one solution that I discussed early on: put it on your calendar to go to the *gemba* — where the work is actually being done. Talk with the actual people doing it, and observe the processes they use to provide patient care. Do this on a consistent and frequent basis. Ask questions. Offer support. If it is a big deal that you showed up, then the wrong message is being sent about why you are there. Staff should be accustomed to your presence at the *gemba*.

I am not minimizing the usefulness of the tools that were described in this book, for they are, of course, excellent tools! I have used them, as described, in three different organizations and with great success. But first, I had to develop the underlying belief system and gain the commitment of leadership for these tools to be effective.

Can we be satisfied with relying on the same old methods to accomplish different results? I expect my doctors to know the latest in healthcare practices, protocols, equipment, etc. Plus attitudes toward providers and hospitals have changed. Patients expect more from healthcare providers than being a mere diagnosis for them to practice their craft upon. Patients, too, have more information to shop around and pick and choose who provides that care, and hospitals are being stretched thin on resources to provide that very care. Shouldn't our management practices also keep up with changing times and expectations?

In this book, I have offered you a blueprint for building the kind of successful healthcare system you want. If you follow it, I am sure you will find it supports your success.

# Appendices

## Appendix A—Generic Meeting Agenda Format

# Meeting Agenda

**Meeting Topic:**
**Date:**
**Time:**
**Location:**

| | TOPIC | PRESENTER | TIME (minutes) | DISCUSS | INFO | FOLLOW-UP | ACTION | STRATEGY | NOTES |
|---|---|---|---|---|---|---|---|---|---|
| 1. | | | | ☐ | ☐ | ☐ | ☐ | | |
| 2. | | | | ☐ | ☐ | ☐ | ☐ | | |
| 3. | | | | ☐ | ☐ | ☐ | ☐ | | |
| 4. | | | | ☐ | ☐ | ☐ | ☐ | | |
| 5. | | | | ☐ | ☐ | ☐ | ☐ | | |
| 6. | | | | ☐ | ☐ | ☐ | ☐ | | |
| 7. | | | | ☐ | ☐ | ☐ | ☐ | | |

**TOTAL TIME:** _____ Minutes

**Next Meeting:** Date: _____ Time: _____ Location: _____

## Appendix B—Facilitated Meeting Agenda Format

# Enterprise Cash Management Tool Work Group
## May 8th, 8:30 am – 12:30 pm, OPEX Learning Center

| Time | Activity | Who |
|------|----------|-----|
| 8:30 (20) | **Agenda**<br>○ Reflection<br>○ Review History & Charter<br>   ○ Cash Management Tool Workshop (April 23-24)<br>   ○ Flow charts<br>   ○ Cash Management Discoveries<br>      ○ Ownership of Cash Management (Proposal coming)<br>      ○ Bank Statements<br>      ○ Cash Drawer Extract<br>      ○ Timing of this work against EPIC<br>○ The Sponsor Team (Doug & Sharon)<br>   ○ Expectations for today's work<br>     1. The team will develop work standards that support the EPIC implementation:<br>       a. Single Bank Statement daily download - Karen indicated finance would own this.<br>       b. What will be the process? Will StE need to change any current process to support this new future state?<br>       c. Document the standards<br>     2. We need an update to the existing StE tool-was the task completed to expand? Is it tested and working? (Cash Drawer Extract, review next steps)<br>     3. We agreed to implement current state cash drawer processes for EPIC as an interim plan.<br>       a. What will this look like?<br>       b. What is the minimum data set for cash control record retention? | Bill & Will |

| | | |
|---|---|---|
| | c. Do we still need to scan copies of checks to the business office? This is the value add versus the non value added analysis.<br>4. Lastly we want to develop a StE Cash Management Committee to oversee the EPIC integration and developing a best practice model for cash controls. | |
| 8:50 (25) | **Introductions/Ice Breaker**<br>○ Introduce self and have everyone introduce themselves, their role and their department.<br>○ Icebreaker (an interesting fact about you that this group doesn't know)<br>○ Ground Rules<br>  ○ Silence pagers and call phones<br>  ○ No side conversations<br>  ○ Silence and absence is consent<br>  ○ Attack process, not people<br>  ○ Better now, perfect later<br>  ○ Listen respectfully<br>  ○ Discuss any additional ground rules or behaviors they would like the group to follow. | Bill & Will |
| 9:15 (30) | **The team will develop work standards that support the EPIC implementation:**<br>• Single Bank Statement daily download - Caroline indicated finance would own this.<br>• What will be the process? Will StE need to change any current process to support this new future state?<br>• Document the standards | |
| 9:45 (15) | **Cash Drawer Extract**<br>• Review next steps | |
| 10:00 (15) | **Break** | |

| | | |
|---|---|---|
| **10:15**<br>**(45)** | **We agreed to implement current state cash drawer processes for EPIC as an interim plan.**<br>• What will this look like?<br>• What is the minimum data set for cash control record retention?<br>• Do we still need to scan copies of checks to the business office? | |
| **11:00**<br>**(30)** | **Develop a StE Cash Management Committee to oversee the EPIC integration and developing a best practice model for cash controls.**<br>• What will the purpose be?<br>• Who are the Stakeholders/Members?<br>• Who will lead?<br>• Meeting logistics (where/when/how often) | |
| **11:30**<br>**(30)** | **Plan for Report out**<br>• Work Standards -<br>  • Single Bank Statement download<br>  • Cash Drawer Extract<br>• Agreements<br>  • Minimum data set for cash control<br>  • Cash Management Committee | |
| **12:00**<br>**(30)** | **Report Out**<br>• Call Sharon | |
| **12:30** | **Finish** | |

## Appendix C — One Day Meeting Agenda Format

# Code STEMI...Door-to-Device Time Improvement Project Agenda
### November 1 8:00 am – 5:00 pm OPEX Learning Center

| Time | Activity | Who |
|------|----------|-----|
| (8:00) | **Agenda**<br>o  Reflection<br>o  Workout overview – use of a lot of different techniques to access our thinking in different ways and to access different styles of thinking<br>o  Introduce Sponsor: Provide the authority (permission) to change things today and the approval of your recommendations at the end of the day<br>o  The Sponsor will be back at 4:00PM to hear your recommendation. | Will<br>Lori<br>OpEx<br>Dept. |
| (8:05)<br>15 | **Sponsor Presentation** (Go over first 3 boxes of Charter)<br>o  Review purpose<br>o  Review charter<br>o  Review the goals<br>o  Set expectations | Dan,<br>President |
| (8:20)<br>20 | **Introductions**<br>o  Introduce self and have everyone introduce themselves, their role and their department. | Will<br>Lori |
| (8:40)<br>15 | **Ground Rules**<br>Start with:<br>o  Silence pagers and call phones<br>o  No side conversations<br>o  Silence and absence is consent<br>o  Attack process, not people<br>o  Better now, perfect later<br>o  Listen respectfully<br><br>o  For the next 5 minutes everyone at their table discuss any additional ground rules or behaviors they would like the group to follow and fill out one item per post-it note | Will<br>Lori |

| | | |
|---|---|---|
| | o Going round robin to each table add any additional ground rules.<br>o The facilitator will ensure that the entire group will support the rule by asking, "Can everyone live with this?" If yes, it will be added to the ground rule, if not, the individual that cannot live with it will propose a second version. The facilitator will seek consensus on any changes. | |
| (8:55)<br>30 | **Background Data and Presentation of Project Information**<br>o Power point slide deck presentation of key data for team awareness and discussion<br>o Group discussion of key points for evaluation of current state processes and projected future state opportunities | Rebecca and Dr. T |
| (9:25)<br>35 | **Process Mapping**<br>o Focus on first and last step of the Door-to-Device process (Receiving Hospital and Referring Hospital)<br>o Facilitator/Group write down steps of the process<br>o May have different versions by hospital<br>o Use front wall in OpEx Learning Center to list each process step at each hospital on specific color sheets (8.5"x11") for their hospital.<br>o Walk through final output for general agreement (If the issue is not directly tied to a process, verify an understanding of the issue.<br>Process Boundaries:<br>First step of process:   Patient arrives to the Emergency Department<br>Last step of process:   Reperfusion device is deployed. | Will<br>Lori<br>Rebecca<br>& Dr. K |
| (10:00)<br>15 | **Break** | |
| (10:15)<br>45 | **Brainstorm Problems**<br>o Identify all of the problems together<br>o For the next 5 minutes, everyone write on post-it notes (one idea per post-it) all of the | Will<br>Lori |

| | | |
|---|---|---|
| | issues, problems and barriers that you are experiencing meeting:<br>"Receiving Hospital":<br>1) Target of ≤ 60 minutes Door-to-Device Time<br>"Referring Hospital":<br>1) Target of ≤ 45 minutes Door-to-Transfer Time<br>2) Target of ≤ 120 minutes Door-to-Device Time<br>○ Going round-robin, each person read aloud one post-it and hand it to your group's facilitator; if others have the same comment, pass that to the facilitator as well.<br>○ As the facilitator collects the post-its, he will put them on the wall into a logical grouping<br>○ After all the post-its have been read aloud, collected and grouped, have the group define the "category" or "header" for that group. | |
| (11:00)<br>15 | **Categorize problems against the process**<br>○ Rank order the results & discuss to identify three categories of issues for next step discussion and evaluation. | Will<br>Lori |
| (11:15)<br>15 | **Prioritize places in the process to make high impact improvements (if needed)**<br>○ Rank order the results & discuss to identify highest priority issues for next step | Will<br>Lori |
| (11:30)<br>30 | **Root Cause Analysis** Divide large group into five person teams for analysis<br>○ 5 Whys (Give example of how to do the 5 Whys)<br>○ For each category or header, ask the questions "Why?" as many times as necessary to determine the root cause. (This might take one or two "whys" or as many as eight.)<br>○ Look for any emerging themes | Will<br>Lori |
| (12:00)<br>45 | **Lunch** | ALL |
| (12:45)<br>45 | **Brainstorm Solutions** | |

167

|  |  |  |
|---|---|---|
|  | o For 5-10 minutes, have the group divide into five person teams to brainstorm solutions onto post-its (one idea per post-it). <br> o Include solutions or counter measures that address the root causes brought forth during the earlier work. <br> o Begin posting solutions on flip charts labeled by category/header from earlier exercise. <br> o The group will need to identify someone to present the data to the other group after lunch. |  |
| (1:30) <br> 30 | **Refine Solutions** <br> o Discuss and agree upon what you want to do <br> **Priority/Payoff Matrix (?)** <br> o Find the solutions that have the highest payoff and are easy to implement |  |
| (2:00) <br> 40 | **Team Report-outs** <br> o Each "five person team" takes 5 minutes to report to other teams to quickly check-in for overlap <br> **Refine Solutions** <br> o Discuss and agree upon what you want to do |  |
| (2:40) <br> 35 | **Action Plan – WWW (Everyone come together as one final group)** <br> o In order to accomplish these countermeasures, several actions needed to be taken, such as training, informing, communicating, enforcing, etc. <br> o For the next 5 minutes, everyone write onto post-it notes (one idea per post-it) all of the actions, in as much detail as possible, that need to be taken. For example, don't write communicate. Write what should be communicated, how it should be communicated, etc. <br> o Include the time frame (week 1, week 2, week 3, etc.) in which the action should be taken <br> o Identify gaps between current state and desired target. |  |

| | | |
|---|---|---|
| | o   Plan action steps for closing gaps.<br>o   Identify one person to present the plan after the break. | |
| (3:15)<br>30 | **Action Plan**<br>o   One person presents the plan<br>o   The rest of the group listen for completeness and agreement<br>o   After the plan has been read aloud, as a group, answer the question, "What changes need to be made?<br>o   Adjust the plan accordingly.<br>o   Prepare the final report out on the power point template | |
| (3:45) | **Break/Prepare for Report Out** | |
| (4:00)<br>50 | **Report Out to SPONSOR and GUESTS**<br>o   Sponsor Assessment and Approval | Sponsor<br>Dan |
| (4:50)<br>10 | **Evaluate the work and process of the day**<br>o   Plus / Delta for the day | Team<br>Members |
| 5:00 | **Closure** | |

169

## Appendix D — Rapid Process Improvement Workshop (a.k.a. Kaizen event) Agenda Format

**Agenda – Rapid Process Improvement Workshop (RPIW)**

**Care Management Across the Continuum of Care — The Shift to a Clinically Integrated Network**

**September 24 – 26**

| Tuesday September, 24 | Wednesday, September 25 | Thursday, September 26 |
|---|---|---|
| 8:00 • Welcome, Opening Reflection, Agenda<br>• Introductions<br>• Ground Rules for our time together<br>• Agenda/Stage Setting<br><br>8:20 • Clarify Purpose – The New Purpose – The Shift to a Clinically Integrated Network – Peter O'Connor<br><br>8:35 • Principles – Patient Centered | 8:00 • What are the signals?<br>• What are the information flows<br>• Action Driven | 8:00 • First steps<br>• Measures of progress<br>• Action Plan<br>   ○ Now – 6 month<br>   ○ 6 – 12 months |
| Lunch 12 - 1 | Lunch 12 - 1 | Lunch 12 - 1 |
| The Model – Stephen<br>• The Staff Lens<br>• The Patient experience<br>• Patient meaning<br>• Staff meaning | Practices New<br>• More of /Less of<br>• New Work Flows | • Plan Report out<br>• Report out |

Appendix E—Charter Format

# Initiative Improvement Team Charter

| | |
|---|---|
| **Title of Project:** | |
| **Department:** | |
| **Campus:** | |
| **Date charter started:** | |
| **Method:** | |

Process Boundaries

| | |
|---|---|
| **Issue/Problem Statement:** | |
| **First Step of Customer Process:** | |
| **Last Step of Customer Process:** | |
| **Includes:** | |
| **Excludes:** | |
| **Potential Barriers** | |
| **Non-negotiable:** | Cannot add FTEs. No capital expenses above $200. Etc. |

## Measures and ROI

| Measure: (Graph with baselines and targets/goals attached) | |
|---|---|
| Sponsor/Team Leader expectation of the "product" for the end of the workshop. What do you want to see at the Report Out? What will a successful workshop look like? | The end of a workshop will include: a solution/recommendation that includes standard work, **and** an implementation plan that includes check and adjust meetings. You want the sponsor to approve both. |

## Participants/Roles

| | |
|---|---|
| Sponsor: | |
| Process Owner(s): | |
| Team Leader/Implementation Manager: | |
| Physician Champion: | |
| Facilitator(s): | |
| Scheduler: | |
| Planning Team Members: | |
| Workshop Attendees / Team Members (Name/Position): | |
| Report Out Guests: | Executive Sponsor, |
| Check / Adjust Start Date; Deliverable; Distribution | |

| (if other than workshop attendees and Team Leader) On-call Resources (Name, Phone #) | |
|---|---|
| | |
| | |

**Signature**

Executive Sponsor:

_____

**Signature**

Karl G Kraber, Facilitator:

_____

## Example Graph – MUST BE REPLACED

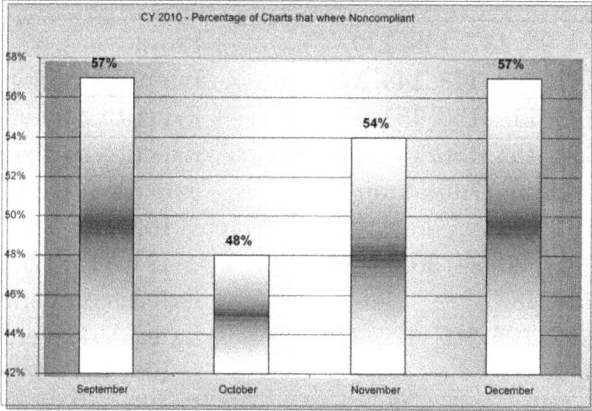

# SIPOC/COPIS

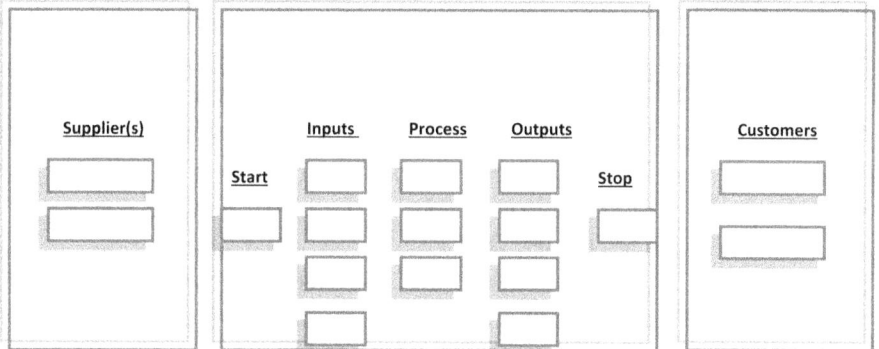

# Index

www.ingramcontent.com/pod-product-compliance
Lightning Source LLC
Chambersburg PA
CBHW071233210326
41597CB00016B/2036